T0044245

The Enigma Girls

**How Ten Teenagers Broke Ciphers, Kept
Secrets, and Helped Win World War II**

The Enigma Girls

**How Ten Teenagers Broke Ciphers, Kept
Secrets, and Helped Win World War II**

Candace Fleming

SCHOLASTIC
FOCUS
NEW YORK

Library of Congress Cataloging-in-Publication Data

Names: Fleming, Candace, author.
Title: The enigma girls : how ten teenagers broke ciphers, kept secrets, and helped win World War II / Candace Fleming.
Description: First edition. | New York : Scholastic Focus, 2024. | Includes bibliographical references and index. | Audience: Ages 7-11 | Audience: Grades 4-6 | Summary: ""You are to report to Station X at Bletchley Park, Buckinghamshire, in four days time....That is all you need to know." This was the terse telegram hundreds of young women throughout the British Isles received in the spring of 1941, as World War II raged. As they arrived at Station X, a sprawling mansion in a state of disrepair surrounded by Spartan-looking huts with little chimneys coughing out thick smoke-these young people had no idea what kind of work they were stepping into. Who had recommended them? Why had they been chosen? Most would never learn all the answers to these questions. Bletchley Park was a well-kept secret during World War II, operating under the code name Station X. The critical work of code-cracking Nazi missives that went on behind its closed doors could determine a victory or loss against Hitler's army. Amidst the brilliant cryptographers, flamboyant debutantes, and absent-minded professors working there, it was teenaged girls who kept Station X running. Some could do advanced math, while others spoke a second language. They ran the unwieldy bombe machines, made sense of wireless sound waves, and sorted the decoded messages. They were expected to excel in their fields and most importantly: know how to keep a secret"— Provided by publisher.
Identifiers: LCCN 2023036019 (print) | LCCN 2023036020 (ebook) | ISBN 9781338749571 (hardback) | ISBN 9781338749588 (ebook)
Subjects: LCSH: Government Code and Cypher School (Great Britain)—Juvenile literature. | Great Britain. Royal Navy. Women's Royal Naval Service (1939-1993)—Biography—Juvenile literature. | World War, 1939-1945—Cryptography—Juvenile literature. | Enigma cipher system—Juvenile literature. | World War, 1939-1945—Military intelligence—Great Britain—Juvenile literature. | Bletchley Park (Milton Keynes, England)—History—Juvenile literature. | BISAC: JUVENILE NONFICTION / Girls & Women | JUVENILE NONFICTION / History / Holocaust
Classification: LCC D810.C88 F54 2024 (print) | LCC D810.C88 (ebook) | DDC 940.54/8641—dc23/eng/20230825
LC record available at https://lccn.loc.gov/2023036019
LC ebook record available at https://lccn.loc.gov/2023036020

10 9 8 7 6 5 4 3 2 1   24 25 26 27 28

Printed in Italy 183

First edition, March 2024

Book design by Stephanie Yang

contents

1942: BOMBES AND CODEBOOKS

1943: SLOGGING, GRINDING WAR WORK

1944: D-DAY AND ITS SECRET HELPERS

Three women at work at the Bombe machines in
Eastcote Outstation in England.

INTRODUCTION

This is the story of a handful of young women—teenagers really—who left their childhoods behind and walked into the unknown. They had no idea where they were going, or what they would be asked to do. They only knew it was wartime, and they wanted to do their bit. With record players and teddy bears in tow, they ended up doing vital, top secret work at a place called Bletchley Park. Certainly, there are bigger names in the history of World War II cipher breaking—Alan Turing, Dilly Knox, Tommy Flowers, and the like have had numerous books written about their remarkable contributions at Bletchley Park. They are heroes. But so, too, are these ten mostly overlooked young women (and thousands more like them) who dedicated themselves to hard work and secrecy. For most of their lives, they never breathed a word about their war experiences. Their stories have largely been forgotten . . . until now.

1939–1945

WAR AND Y

WAR!

Poland was just stretching awake on that first day of September 1939. Golden sunlight spread over fields of ripening corn and villages of straw-thatched log houses. Suddenly, the pink horizon grew dark with airplanes—one thousand of them. They flew so low that those on the ground could see their painted crosses and swastikas. Nazis! Bullets and bombs rained from the sky. The noise was deafening—the boom of explosions, the groan of collapsing buildings, shouts and screams. Black smoke blotted out the sun. The hot growing rush of flames was everywhere.

Meanwhile, 1.5 million German soldiers swarmed across the Polish border. The Polish army was no match for the Nazi war machine. This was *blitzkrieg*—lightning warfare.

German troops march victoriously into Warsaw, Poland, after the city's surrender on September 28, 1939.

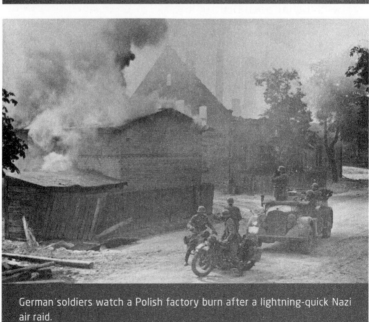

German soldiers watch a Polish factory burn after a lightning-quick Nazi air raid.

Swift, focused, and using an overwhelming force, the Nazis easily overran Poland. Soon, Germany's ruthless dictator, Adolf Hitler, would rule this country. But invading Poland was just a first step in Hitler's larger plan to conquer *all* of Europe. Someday, he believed, Paris would be his. So would London. And no one would be able to stop him.

In Britain, Prime Minister Neville Chamberlain was both stunned and furious. A year earlier, after seizing Czechoslovakia, Hitler had signed an agreement with Britain promising not to grab any more territory. Now he'd broken that promise—reason enough to declare war. But matters were made worse by the fact that both Britain and France had signed an agreement with Poland promising to come to its defense if it was ever attacked. What could Chamberlain do? He gave Hitler an ultimatum: Pull out of Poland immediately, or Britain and France would declare war. Hitler had until eleven o'clock on the morning of September 3 to respond.

Hour after tense hour passed.

All of Europe waited.

At eleven a.m. on Sunday, September 3, citizens across the British Empire gathered around their radios to hear a special announcement from Prime Minister Chamberlain. Was it war?

Chamberlain came on. His voice was grave. Hitler had ignored his ultimatum, leaving England with no choice. "This country is at war," he said. No people—or country—could feel safe in the face of Nazi aggression. The Germans had to be stopped. Europe must be saved. "For it is evil things that we shall be fighting against," he concluded, "brute force, bad faith, injustice, oppression and persecution; and against them I am certain that right will prevail."

Fearing the Germans would drop poison gas bombs on Britain, the British government passed out gas masks to every citizen. Here, a nursery school class practices using them.

A view of London's famous clock, Big Ben, from behind barbed wire. Barbed wire was used to both protect important structures and snare potential enemies.

The country quickly mobilized. Blackout was strictly enforced. This meant that the windows and doors of all buildings were tightly covered at night to prevent any glimmer of light that might aid enemy aircraft during night bombings. Sandbags were placed in front of doors, and trenches were dug in parks. Gas masks were handed out like candy, and air raid shelters cropped up in small towns and city neighborhoods. London looked especially strange as barrage balloons—blimps on wires to keep low-flying aircraft from attacking at close range—filled the city's sky. Even the wrought-iron fences around the country's cemeteries and public squares were pulled out and melted down for munitions.

Men and women wearing uniforms were suddenly everywhere. So were ration cards. The German navy had begun sinking ships headed for Britain that were carrying essential goods like grains, sugar, meat, and gasoline. As these goods grew scarce, rationing was set up as a way of guaranteeing that everyone got his or her fair share. The British government now limited citizen consumption of butter, sugar, meat, canned milk, shoes, gasoline, silk, rubber, and more.

Meanwhile, officials began moving important government agencies out into the countryside in hopes they'd be

BLACKOUT TIME
TO-NIGHT IS AT

Mandatory nightly blackouts were monitored by a local citizen volunteer known as an "air raid precautions warden." Here, one such warden adjusts a public sign indicating what time everything should go black.

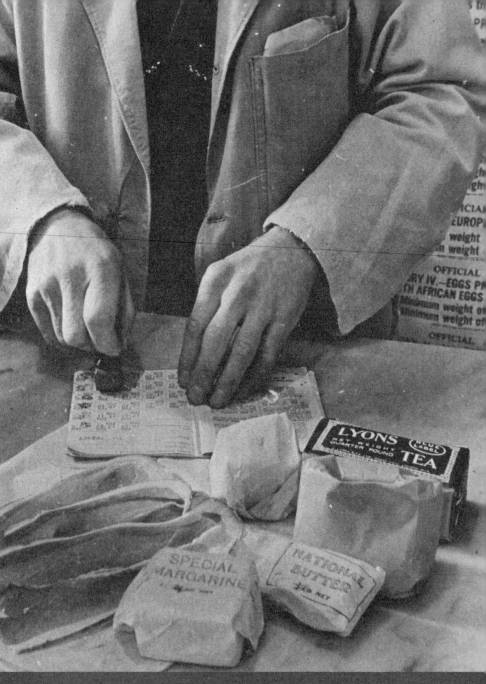

The British government issued every citizen a ration card with coupons. These coupons were used to buy rationed food items. The fixed amount for each person per week was one egg, two ounces of tea and butter, an ounce of cheese, eight ounces of sugar, and four ounces of bacon and margarine. Here, a grocer stamps the ration coupons in a book, indicating that the customer has bought his or her allotment for the week.

safe from bomber raids. One of these agencies was the Government Code and Cipher School (GC&CS). An arm of the Secret Intelligence Service, GC&CS's job was code breaking. And its very existence was hush-hush. Packing up their files and equipment, the small team of code breakers slipped out of London. They set up their new base of operation in a redbrick manor house located on a country estate fifty miles away.

The estate was called Bletchley Park.

Code name: Station X.

Here the team gathered intelligence of the most crucial nature. They strove to outwit the Nazis and break into German codes and ciphers. If they succeeded, they would be able to penetrate to the very heart of the enemy's operations. What was Hitler planning? Where were German troops? What kind of equipment was being used? Intelligence like *that* could save lives. It could affect how commanders fought battles. Above all, it could win the war.

2

SECRET LISTENERS

Something suspicious was going on at the St. Leonard's Hotel. A dozen young women—mostly in their late teens or early twenties—had moved into the cliffside building on the outskirts of Withernsea, and completely taken it over. Sometimes, the locals in this tiny coastal village caught a glimpse of the young women riding their bicycles, or sunbathing on the beach. But most of the time, they stuck close to the hotel. Obviously, they lived *and* worked there.

Even more suspicious was the forest of tall radio antennas that sprouted up alongside the hotel. The villagers speculated. It was all very curious. Few of them, however, guessed the truth: The St. Leonard's Hotel had been converted into a secret listening station. And the teenagers were eavesdropping on the enemy.

One of these secret listeners was eighteen-year-old Patricia Owtram. Her ears clamped in headphones, she sat before her wireless radio equipment. The glow from its illuminated dials cast a golden hue onto her face as she listened to the airwaves' hissing static. With her right hand, she slowly turned the big dial at the radio's center back and forth, back and forth . . . searching. Sometimes she would make out distant and fleeting voices. More often, though, she heard the dots and dashes of Morse code.

These were enemy radio transmissions—a constant stream of them—being broadcast across vast distances. Consider all the enemy aircraft in the sky, all the battalions on land, all the ships and submarines at sea. Each crowded the airwaves with the electronic beeps of Morse code. This was how the Nazis communicated with each other; how they sent weather reports, battle strategy, orders to attack, and more.

Patricia's radio was tuned to German naval traffic in the Baltic and North Seas. Most of the time she listened for Nazi torpedo boats and destroyers that laid sea mines and attacked British ships. Sometimes she picked up a strong

An up-close look at a wireless radio like Patricia's currently on display at the Bletchley Park Trust Archives Museum.

signal, meaning the vessel was close. Other times thick fog banks muffled the signal. And once in a while, she heard signals from far off, like the time she picked up traffic from a German battleship seven hundred miles away.

Now she heard a whooshing sound. She knew what it was: a warming-up signal. German radio operators switched on their radios several minutes before transmitting any messages.

Patricia stopped. Listened. Moved her radio dial.

She knew the radio operator was out there, somewhere in the North Atlantic, preparing to send information that would aid his fellow Nazis. Patricia tried to remember that behind the dots and dashes was a human being. Was the German radio operator also a teenager? Had the war drastically changed his life, too?

Just months earlier, Patricia had been living with her family in a rural Lancashire village. Like many young women, she'd believed the course of her life was already mapped out: finish secondary school (England's equivalent of high school), perhaps work for a short time in an office, then meet a nice young man, get married, and have children. But with war, Patricia saw a new path. She decided to join the Women's Royal Naval Service (commonly called the Wrens). The Wrens accepted volunteers starting at age seventeen (younger with parental consent). In truth, Patricia had just a vague idea of what Wrens did. She picked the organization because it had a stylish uniform—white blouse, blue skirt, and an attractive ribbon-trimmed hat.

Few Wrens actually went to sea. Instead, new volunteers were sent to the Royal Naval Academy, where they were assessed and trained for jobs such as meteorologist, secretary, or bomb maker.

"Can you stay awake all night?" a naval officer asked Patricia.

The teenager answered yes.

And so she was posted as a radio operator.

Over the next six weeks, Patricia learned radio procedure and Morse code. She also adjusted to her new life. She'd never been away from home before. Indeed, she'd rarely traveled. She felt bewildered and frightened, tossed into the unknown with girls from all walks of life and backgrounds. Had she made a mistake joining up? It was too late to wonder. She was already on an unknown adventure to help the war effort. With her training complete, she was sent to the St. Leonard's Hotel in Withernsea.

She'd been here three weeks now.

Under the watchful eye of instructors, Wrens train for the Y service. Here they are learning to take down messages sent via Morse code.

Tonight—her first on the four a.m. to eight a.m. shift—she sat motionless, ears straining, waiting for the German radio operator to start transmitting. Her head tipped to one side. She was as alert as a cat at a mouse hole.

The Nazis knew that hundreds of British citizens, just like Patricia, were listening in with the goal of discovering their military plans. In the months leading up to the war, the British government had established a web of intercept sites, called Y stations. Y stations could be found in such far-flung places as Singapore, Hong Kong, and Australia (all part of the British empire at the time), as well as along Britain's east and west coasts. The government created these stations by commandeering farmhouses, manor homes, and hotels like St. Leonard's. The Nazis, however, weren't overly concerned about these listening stations. German High Command believed they'd come up with an impenetrable way of sending radio messages: the Enigma cipher machine.

At first glance, the Enigma machine looked like a typewriter sitting in a wooden box. Like a typewriter, it had a keyboard with one key for each letter of the alphabet. (There were no numbers or punctuation marks.) This, however, was where the similarity ended. Behind the keyboard sat a lamp

An up-close look at a German Enigma machine.

board with a series of lights that corresponded to the letters on the keyboard. And underneath the keyboard was a plug board with six double sockets. These sockets corresponded to both the keyboard and the lamp board. Additionally, inside the machine were three gears, or rotors, that could be

A German Enigma machine with its three rotors removed.

removed and replaced. Around the edges of these rotors were the letters of the alphabet.

To encrypt a message on the Enigma, the operator set up his machine according to the secret instructions he received each day from German High Command. These predetermined positions were called settings. To do this, he first put the rotors into the machine in the specified order. Next, he moved each rotor to that day's starting letter. He then typed each letter of the message into the machine using the keyboard. With each key press, an electrical impulse passed through the machine, turning the rotors and lighting up the encrypted letter on the lamp board.

But the lit-up letter was not the same letter that was pressed. For example, if the operator pressed the K key, it was not the letter K that lit up on the lamp board. Instead, it might have been an L or maybe a P. If the operator struck the K a second time, an entirely different letter lit up. In fact, the only letter that wouldn't have lit up in this instance *was* K. That was because on Enigma, a pressed key never illuminated itself.

Since the Enigma did not print anything out, the operator had to write down the encrypted letter from the lamp board before typing in the next letter, and the next, and so

German Enigma operators in the field. The first operator (center) keys in the original message while the second operator (left) takes down the encrypted letters. Once the entire message is encrypted, he will translate it into Morse code. Then the first operator will send it on.

on until the entire message was encrypted. And the number of different ways it could be encrypted was mind-boggling. Between the rotors and the plug board, a typical Enigma had 159 quintillion possible combinations. Was it any wonder the Germans believed the ciphers generated by an Enigma machine were unbreakable? It would have taken a cryptographer, a person who breaks ciphers, more than a lifetime to go through all the possible combinations.

A second Enigma operator converted the encrypted letters into Morse code. He then transmitted them in blocks of four or five letters over his wireless radio.

Patricia was still listening. Suddenly, the hissing airwaves gave way to the staccato beat of Morse code. Dot, dash, dot, dot! Adrenaline shot through her.

Swiftly, she wrote out the letters exactly as she heard them, simultaneously converting them from Morse code into plain text. Her fingers cramped as she hurried to keep up, tearing pieces of paper off specially lined notepads, scribbling like mad with her pencil. She knew she had just one chance to pluck the letters from the airwaves. And she had to be accurate. A lost or misheard signal could cost lives. Had she gotten it right? She would never know. She couldn't understand

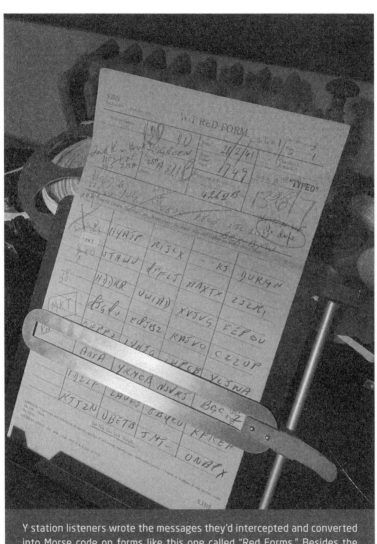

Y station listeners wrote the messages they'd intercepted and converted into Morse code on forms like this one called "Red Forms." Besides the enciphered text, Red Forms also included the frequency on which the message was heard, as well as the date and time.

the message. It was nothing but a meaningless scramble of encrypted letters:

UKCPA JMBOP GFLXW EJMIK XNZDY

But the Nazi who received the message would understand. Like Patricia, he, too, converted the letters from Morse code into plain text. He, too, ended up with gibberish. But he had an Enigma machine calibrated to that day's settings. One by one, he typed in the encrypted letters. One by one, the real letters were illuminated on his machine's lamp board. He wrote each letter down. The message slowly became clear. What did it say?

That was what the British needed to find out.

Patricia's shift ended with the rising sun. Handing her headphones to her replacement, she stood and stretched. She did not know that she'd been transcribing Enigma ciphers. The high levels of security surrounding her work meant she was given only enough information to do her job, nothing more. She glanced at the stack of enemy communications. Where were they headed?

Patricia knew only its code name: Station X.

If You Were a Code and Cipher Cracker: Codes vs. Ciphers

Let's start with the basics. There are two kinds of secret writing: **codes** and **ciphers**.

A **code** is a form of writing in which each individual word is written as a secret code word, code number, or code symbol. Here, for example, is part of a code used by American generals during World War II:

For the word TROOPS use WHITE
For the word CANNON use YELLOW
For the word BRIDGE use PURPLE
For the word ORDER use BLACK
For the word TO use PINK.

An army commander could encode (put a message into a secret code) these orders and send them to field officers like this:

BLACK WHITE YELLOW PINK PURPLE

Only an army officer who knew the code would be able to decode (read an encoded message by using the secret code) the commander's orders:

ORDER TROOPS AND CANNON TO BRIDGE

(Unimportant words like "and" are usually omitted if the message is perfectly clear without them.)

Codes are hard to break. Doing so means figuring out the meaning of every code word, number, or symbol. But codes also have one big drawback: They require a codebook because there are just too many code words, numbers, or symbols to remember. If that codebook is lost or stolen, the person who found or swiped it can read any message that is sent. For this reason, the military turned to ciphers.

A **cipher** is a system of secret writing in which every *letter*, instead of every word, has its own secret symbol. If you are

enciphering a message, you are putting it into a secret cipher. If you are **deciphering** a message, you are reading an enciphered message by using the secret cipher.

The most common cipher is an alphabet cipher. This type of cipher uses a code letter for each letter of the words in the real message. There are many kinds of alphabet ciphers. Here is one used two thousand years ago by the famous Roman general Julius Caesar:

First, print the alphabet. Then at the end of the alphabet, also print the first two letters of a second alphabet like this:

ABCDEFGHIJKLMNOPQRSTUVWXYZAB

Now write your message beneath the alphabet:

ABCDEFGHIJKLMNOPQRSTUVWXYZAB
HELLO

Next, find the letter H in the alphabet. Move two letters to the right. This is the letter J, and it will be the first letter in your enciphered message. Below the letter H write the letter J:

ABCDEFGHIJKLMNOPQRSTUVWXYZAB

HELLO

J

Below the letter E write the second letter after E, which is G.

ABCDEFGHIJKLMNOPQRSTUVWXYZAB

HELLO

JG

Do the same for the other three letters in your message. When you've finished, your enciphered message will be:

JGNNQ

What if you received this message? How would you decipher it? It would be easy if you knew the key to the cipher. You would simply print an alphabet with two extra letters at the end so that if the A or B appear in the message you would be able to count back from those letters. Next, you would write the message below the extra-long alphabet. Then you would count *back* two letters. You would come to the letter

H. Write H below the J. Then count back two letters from G and write E, etc.

But what if you didn't know the cipher? Could you break into the secret message? Maybe . . . eventually . . . with lots of trial and error.

Of course, people sending secret communications know that ciphers get broken. And so they change their cipher. In this case, if you thought someone had figured out your cipher, you could change it by moving ahead three letters, or four letters, or ten.

This would make deciphering your messages even harder.

The Nazis know all of this, of course. They, too, will use an alphabet cipher—an extraordinarily sophisticated version. And they will change the key to that cipher every single day of the war.

1940

SECRETS, SECRETS,
AND MORE SECRETS

3

JANE

Eighteen-year-old Jane Hughes wanted to do her bit to defeat Hitler. But how? Could she work in a munitions factory, making bullets or bombs? Could she learn to drive an ambulance? Thousands of British girls were signing on to do essential war work. Jane longed to join them.

But her parents, Lord and Lady Hughes, wouldn't hear of it. War work? Oh, no! Their daughter had far more important things to do. In just a few weeks—wearing a white ball gown, long gloves, and feathers in her specially coiffed hair—Jane was expected to gracefully descend Buckingham Palace's grand staircase. At the bottom, she would curtsy to King George VI and Queen Elizabeth. This was a ritual set

As more and more men were called up, women filled the work shortages at home. Female ambulance drivers, like these two working to free their vehicle from the mud, were crucial, often transporting the wounded at night and in unsafe conditions. Their bravery and dedication saved thousands of lives.

Almost one million women worked in munitions factories during the war, making weapons like shells and bullets. These three women have trained to become welders, a particularly dangerous and labor-intensive job.

in stone. For generations, the teenage daughters of Britain's upper class—called debutantes—had "come out" to high society in this manner. War or no war, the proprieties still held.

Jane dreaded it. What a complete waste of time. The palace ball marked the beginning of "the Season," a months-long whirlwind of parties, dances, and dinners. Lady Hughes insisted the Season would launch Jane into grown-up life. But Jane knew its real purpose: to introduce her to marriageable young men. And Jane wanted none of it—not the dancing, nor the queen. Most of all, she did not want the husband.

A debutante ball like the kind Jane's parents wanted her to attend.

Then, out of the blue, Jane received a letter. How odd! It was from Elizabeth Blandy, a schoolmate Jane hadn't spoken with in years. Odder still was Elizabeth's request. She wrote:

Well, Jane, I'm at Bletchley and it's perfectly frightful. We're so overworked, so desperately busy. You must come and join us.

Bletchley? The tiny village was best known as a place people passed through on their way to busier, bigger towns. It did, however, have one notable feature—Bletchley Park, a fifty-three-acre country estate complete with a sprawling mansion and man-made lake. Still, the place was in the absolute boon-docks! What was wealthy, well-educated Elizabeth doing way out there? Curiosity seized Jane. She *had* to find out.

Days later, she took the train to Bletchley. Uniformed sol-diers en route to training camps and military bases crammed every compartment, and the hour-long trip seemed to take an age. At last, she stepped out onto Bletchley's railroad sta-tion platform. She shivered in the wintry March air. The town was a hodgepodge of redbrick houses and thatched cottages. A pub sat on the high street, along with two movie theaters and a string of small shops selling hats, cakes, and secondhand furniture. Jane would later learn that one could buy a live chicken at Bletchley's weekly cattle market, as well as worship at one of its five churches. A row of chimneys from the village's brick factory belched black soot over everything.

Jane picked her way along a gravel path. Bletchley Park came into view. An eight-foot fence topped by a curl of barbed wire surrounded its perimeter, and a guardhouse had been built at the main gates. Military police looked at her suspi-ciously. Not allowed in without a pass, Jane waited outside the gates until Elizabeth appeared to escort her inside.

Strange! A small wooden building had been built where a rose garden had obviously once been. Other buildings, too,

Bletchley's train station as it looked at the time of Jane's arrival.

The village of Bletchley, c. 1940.

freckled the estate grounds. Even more strange, the place swarmed with men and women, some in uniform, some dressed in civilian clothing. What were they all doing here?

Elizabeth refused to say. Instead, she explained how she'd come to be at Bletchley Park. Friends of her wealthy father had recommended her. From one of Britain's best families, Elizabeth was considered a "suitable girl." Her background made her trustworthy in the eyes of Park officials.

Trustworthy meant she could keep secrets.

Park officials asked her if she knew any other "suitable girls." And Elizabeth had immediately thought of Jane.

Jane bubbled with curiosity as she followed her friend around an ornamental lake and down a winding path to one of the wooden buildings. Elizabeth called it "Hut 6." She led Jane into one of its rooms and left her there alone.

The hut's walls were bare, and blackout curtains covered the windows. Because it was daytime, they'd been left open to let in the fading spring light. Still, the room remained dim. Only a single light bulb hanging from the ceiling gave off any illumination.

The door opened and a man entered.

Jane recognized him immediately—Stuart Milner-Barney, the famous chess player. What was he doing here?

A view across Bletchley Park's ornamental lake to the manor house.

She didn't know that Milner-Barney had himself only recently arrived at Bletchley Park, handpicked because of his incredible ability to think ahead and work out strategies. She didn't know that others with unique talents and skills—mathematicians, Egyptologists, those good at crossword puzzles, language specialists—had also been secretly recruited to work at the Park.

Milner-Barney stared at her. She stared back. An uncomfortable silence fell. Obviously, he was supposed to interview her. But it was also obvious that he didn't know how. Finally, he muttered something about taking Jane over to see his boss, Commander Edward Travis, who was the deputy director of Bletchley Park.

They headed toward the Victorian-styled mansion that sat in the middle of the estate. Its main entrance was oak paneled and spacious, with rooms branching off each side. In the front hall, a copy of the London *Times* listing that day's fatalities had been pinned to a pegboard. In woeful silence, a handful of people read it. Milner-Barney led her up a grand staircase into what had once been a bay-windowed bedroom, but was now a private office.

Commander Travis looked up from his desk. So she had come for the job, eh? It would be vital to the war effort, he told her. His voice grew stern. "What I am going to say [Miss Hughes] is extremely important. You will be working in the most secret place in Britain, and all the activities here are crucial to the war. The work here is so secret that you will be told only what is necessary for you to know, and you will never, never seek to find out more."

He paused, letting his words sink in. Then he continued, "You will never mention the name of this place, not to your family, not to your friends, not to anyone you may meet. . . . You will never disclose to anyone the nature of the work you will be doing. Nor will you mention anything about the location of this place. . . . You can tell your family you are doing ordinary clerical work, and you will never discuss with anyone outside your own section the work you will be doing."

"And what work will that be, sir?" Jane asked.

Commander Travis looked as if he were about to explode. "Good God, girl," he exclaimed. "Haven't you listened to a single thing I've said? I know nothing about your work, and I don't want to know anything."

Then he opened his desk and pulled out a document. "This is the Official Secrets Act. It clearly states that if you disclose the slightest information about this place or your work . . . you will be committing TREASON."

This was strong stuff for an eighteen-year-old, and Jane was nervously impressed.

"If you did," he added, "you would be liable to the most extreme penalties of the law. . . . I'm not sure whether, at this moment, that's hanging or shooting by firing squad."

Was he joking? He didn't look it. He handed her a fountain pen and motioned for her to sign the document.

Jane did. It was the spontaneous act of an eighteen-year-old. She had no clue what she'd just signed. In fact, the Official Secrets Act bound her to a lifetime of secrecy. She could never, *ever* talk about her work at the Park. Not even after she left, and not for the rest of her life.

That evening, she told her parents that she'd gotten a job.

They were stunned. "Well, where are you going?"

"Clerical work," she quickly replied. It was all she could tell them.

She did, however, give them an address where they could write her. For security reasons, it wasn't Bletchley Park's real address, but rather a post office box in London. Her parents wouldn't be able to visit or call her, either, although she was allowed to phone them. And every few weeks, she'd get "leave," or days off. She'd try to visit then.

Her parents accepted the situation without argument. They didn't even press for more information. Since the start of the war, the government had urged citizens

Just one of many posters plastered across Britain warning citizens not to talk, or ask questions about the war.

to stifle discussions and speculation. Posters that read CARE-
LESS TALK COSTS LIVES had sprung up everywhere. It was
widely understood that one should not ask questions, or
discuss more than was necessary.

Still, Lady Hughes must have been disappointed about the
palace ball.

The following Monday, Jane returned to Bletchley Park,
and Hut 6. At last, Stuart Milner-Barney explained her job.
Alongside thirty others—most of them male mathematics students recruited from Cambridge, Oxford, and other
British universities—she would be helping to break Enigma
ciphers. Hut 6 was dedicated solely to the encrypted communications sent by the Luftwaffe (the German air force)
and the Wehrmacht (the German army). Each had its own
Enigma network. And the settings for their machines, also
known as keys, changed every day. It was these settings that
cryptographers were trying to figure out. How did they do it?

Everything started with the intercepted messages, or
intercepts, that came into Hut 6 from the Y stations. These
were logged in the Registration Room by a group of young
women who sorted them into two groups—Luftwaffe or

A modern-day look at Hut 6 (right) and Hut 3 (directly behind it).

Wehrmacht. They noted the number of letters in each message, the place it had originated, and on what radio frequency it was sent.

The intercepts then went to the Machine Room, where most of the mathematicians worked. Jane and the others called them the "boffins," or geniuses. One of the Hut 6 boffins could do the London *Times* crossword puzzle without writing in a single clue. He could just see it all in his head. Others were so preoccupied with cipher breaking, they sometimes came to work in the oddest assortment of clothing: "old overcoats tied shut with string, wooly hats made from tea

The Registration Room in Hut 6, c. 1940.

cozies and sometimes pajama trousers showing beneath their everyday clothes." They huddled over the messages, pencils in hand, trying to find the settings. They used cribs—snippets of messages deduced through educated guesses—and other cryptanalytical strategies that Jane didn't understand. If one of the boffins believed he'd worked out a setting, he moved to the Enigma machine in the corner (this was the reason it was called the Machine Room) and tested his solution. If the message was no longer gibberish, but instead came out in plain German text, he knew he was right.

How had Bletchley Park gotten its hands on an Enigma machine? It had come from Poland, through secret channels. Years earlier, the Polish government—feeling dangerously squeezed between Nazi Germany and Soviet Russia—had set up a top secret organization called the Polish Cipher Bureau. The Bureau's main purpose was to crack Enigma. After all, if Poland had any chance of protecting itself, it needed intelligence. It had to know what Germany and Russia were up

The boffins in Hut 6 trying to crack the day's Enigma settings, c. 1940.

to. Polish cryptologists worked doggedly. Through spy networks, they eventually uncovered the workings of the Enigma machine. Having discovered the crucial wiring of the individual rotors, they built their own Enigma machines. In 1939, however, with war looming, they decided to share what they knew with the British. This included giving them one of the three Enigma machines they'd built.

Once the boffin in Hut 6 had determined that he'd worked out the setting, all that day's messages using that particular setting could then be deciphered. This further

A close-up look at a Typex like the kind Jane worked on.

deciphering, however, was not done by the boffin. That would have been an incredible waste of his time. After all, there wasn't just a single Enigma cipher. The German army, navy, and air force operated their Enigma machines on their own, with different ciphers depending on where they were fighting. This meant that every day, dozens of settings needed to be cracked.

Instead, the stacks of encrypted messages were sent to the Decoding Room, where Jane, along with four or five other girls, worked. The girls didn't have Enigma machines. Instead, they each had a British cipher machine called a Typex, which had been specially converted to work like an Enigma machine. Typexes were clunky plastic-and-steel typewriters that had extra cogs sprouting from their sides and a reel containing a long, thin strip of paper on top. First, the machines were adjusted to the settings discovered by the boffins. Then the letters of the enciphered messages were typed in and the deciphered message came out on the paper strip. One final step remained: The paper strip was cut and glued to the back of the original intercepted message.

Most of the young women in the Decoding Room recognized German text. But Jane could read it. As a sixteen-year-old, she'd lived in Switzerland with a German-speaking family. She still spoke the language fluently. So sometimes, as she typed, she read.

Admittedly, at first it had been hard to do. When the messages emerged from the Typex, they were bunched into groups of five letters without the correct word breaks, like this:

NICHT SZUBE RICHT ENAXA

But over time, she'd gotten the hang of it. In fact, it was like a game, trying to separate the letters into German words. She found she was good at it. In her head, a message like the one above became:

NICHTS ZU BERICHTEN

Translated into English, that meant:

NOTHING TO REPORT

This mental activity helped pass the time as she churned through piles of intercepts.

The deciphered messages—known as decrypts—went to

Hut 6 (left) and Hut 3 (right) were built just feet from one another, as this modern-day photograph shows.

Hut 3, where they were translated into English. The information gleaned from them was assessed and analyzed. Should it be passed on? If so, to whom? Sometimes an officer from Hut 3 would come through the Decoding Room looking for a duplicate or missing message. More often than not, the two huts communicated by means of a shoebox-sized tunnel that connected them. When the decrypts were ready to be passed on, Jane's supervisor put them in a box and used a broom handle to push them through the tunnel. Although it was mere steps away, no one from Hut 6 was allowed to personally deliver anything to Hut 3. *Not ever.* Everyone employed at the Park had to stay within their own work boundaries;

to go into other huts was forbidden unless one had security clearance. And only top brass and boffins had that.

There were, however, a few exceptions to this rule. You could go to Hut 2, where tea with powdered milk and horrid, hard scones were served. If you were ill, you could head to the sick bay in Hut 1. You could also go to the administration hut with permission, or the mansion for dining and recreation, or because you'd been summoned. But everyplace else was strictly off-limits.

Jane often wondered what was happening in Huts 5, 7, 9, and 11. She'd noticed that Huts 8 and 4 were connected in the same way Huts 6 and 3 were. She didn't know, of course, that Hut 8 was breaking Enigma ciphers, too—ones generated by the German Navy, or Kriegsmarine. They sent their decrypts to Hut 4 for translation and intelligence analysis.

Deciphering Enigma communication was a slow, exacting process. On many days, no matter how hard they tried, the boffins could not crack them. Then the Typex machines fell gloomily silent. No decrypts were passed to Hut 3. No intelligence was passed on to the military. And British servicemen had no advance warning of Nazi movements. Were soldiers dying because of it? The thought haunted Jane and her colleagues.

MAVIS

On a dreary day in March, eighteen-year-old Mavis Lever dragged her brown cardboard suitcase aboard the train, and looked around for an available seat. Soldiers filled every compartment. The crush made Mavis feel nervous. *More* nervous. Mavis already felt edgy.

Weeks earlier, she'd quit school, eager to do her bit for the war. She'd considered training as a nurse. But that was before the enlistment officer had learned she spoke German. "We've more important duties for you," he'd said.

He had sounded so mysterious. The teenager's imagination had whirled. She pictured herself parachuting behind enemy lines to steal top secret German documents.

Instead, the enlistment officer handed her a train ticket and gave her these instructions: Catch the 10:40 train from London's Euston Station in four days' time. Get off at Bletchley Station.

But what was she supposed to tell her parents? She lived with them. In fact, she'd never lived anywhere else.

"War work" came the terse reply.

Like Jane's parents, the Levers accepted this short answer without question. So would the parents of thousands of other young women during the course of the war. A desperate unity had been forged by the threat of Nazi invasion, and few people questioned authority. If the government needed their daughters, that was that.

Now, Mavis's train rumbled into Bletchley Station. As instructed, the teenager got off. She walked the half mile to the Park's gates, where one of the guards checked her name off a list. Then he escorted her to the mansion and into Commander Travis's office.

Mavis glanced around. The big house was far different from the ordinary, middle-class home she'd come from.

Travis waved her into a chair, and Mavis dutifully sat. She waited for him to explain why she was there.

Instead, he stressed the importance of secrecy. She could

never tell anyone where she worked. She could never talk about what she was working on. She would go to jail if she did. He pulled a yellowish sheet of paper from his desk drawer—the Official Secrets Act.

Mavis signed it.

Then she trailed after the guard once more, out of the mansion and toward three brick cottages joined together in a single, whitewashed unit. This was where she would work. But doing what? She still didn't know.

Mavis stepped inside "Cottage 3," as it was called. Eight

Cottage 3 as it looks today.

young women sat at a high table, bent over a pile of papers. Beside the window lounged a middle-aged man wearing horn-rimmed glasses and puffing absent-mindedly on a pipe. Mavis couldn't help but notice that his trousers were held up with a piece of twine rather than a belt. When he saw her, he grinned. "We're breaking [ciphers]," he exclaimed. "Have you got a pencil?"

With no further instructions, he handed her a batch of

Dilly Knox.

Enigma encrypted messages and said, "Have a go."

Mavis looked at the dizzying sets of letters. She couldn't make heads or tails of them. "I'm afraid it's all Greek to me," she finally said.

The man laughed heartily. "I wish it were."

The man, Mavis soon learned, was Alfred "Dilly" Knox, a distinguished Greek scholar who'd spent years successfully deciphering ancient papyri fragments at the British Museum. He'd also had a remarkable career as a pioneering cryptographer. He'd handpicked this group of women to break into the Italian Navy's Enigma signals.

Italian? Mavis didn't speak the language.

That didn't matter to Dilly Knox. He believed people who spoke multiple languages—even if that language was German rather than Italian—better understood word patterns and syllables. In fact, he thought breaking a cipher was a lot like a word game. Don't obsess about it, he advised. Don't stare it down. Use "chopped logic." This was Knox's term for looking at things from a new perspective.

One afternoon, weeks after her arrival, Mavis was at the high table. She still didn't get it. She still saw nothing but gibberish. Maybe she wasn't cut out for this type of work.

"Which way does a clock go round?" Knox asked her.

"Clockwise," she answered.

"Oh, no it doesn't," Knox replied, "not if you're the clock. Then it's the opposite way."

And *that*, Mavis realized, was how she had to think about the Enigma machine. She had to consider what was going on *inside* it—the press of its keys, the shift of its rotors, its electrical impulses. But it was so hard. Weeks of solid concentration had led to nothing. The other girls in the Cottage seemed to be making progress. But Mavis was stymied. There was something on the other side of the cipher's curtain, she could feel it, but she couldn't get there. Not yet. She needed chopped logic.

5

LIGHTNING WAR

It happened with lightning speed. On April 9, Germany attacked Denmark. Morning mist mingled with the smoke clouds from Nazi planes as troops swarmed over the border. The Danish army was no match for Hitler's. In less than six hours, Denmark fell.

The German army rolled on, occupying Norway by May 10, before turning westward.

The Netherlands.

Luxembourg.

Belgium.

Each country fell, one after another, like boulders rolling off a cliff.

Initially, French commanders, along with their British allies, believed the Nazis would attack France through Belgium as they had in World War I. But the Germans surprised them by coming through the dense Ardennes Forest in southwest Belgium, a route the French mistakenly believed was impassable. With speed and ferocity, German troops overwhelmed France's defenses. On June 14, they marched into Paris. Hitler was overjoyed.

A Parisian man weeps as he watches Nazi troops march into Paris.

The British watched in horror. The question was no longer *if* the Nazis would cross the English Channel. The question was *when*. That narrow strip of water—just twenty-one miles wide—was all that separated them from the enemy.

A victorious Adolf Hitler poses in front of the Eiffel Tower, the beloved symbol of France, on June 23, 1940. He now viewed the city's treasures as his own.

6

BILLETING BLUES

Chaos! Inside the tiny house, two screeching boys ran up and down the narrow staircase. In the kitchen, their mother banged the breakfast pots while her husband listened to a radio program at full volume.

Lying upstairs on a narrow cot in her cupboard-sized bedroom, Jane tried to sleep. She'd just come off a long, hectic night shift, and was expected back at work in less than eight hours. She needed quiet.

The boys flung open her door. They giggled and poked out their tongues.

This was impossible. Jane couldn't live here. She had to find a different billet.

Billet was the military's word for temporary housing. At Bletchley Park, a special department had been set up to search out lodging for its ever-growing number of workers. Billeting officers went door-to-door, searching for every available room in the patchwork of local villages and country estates surrounding the Park. Anyone with a spare room had to give it up. Many of the locals grumbled about this, but it was mandatory. They had no choice but to open their doors to a complete stranger. In return, they were paid a stipend for each person they accommodated. Some of these lodgings were comfortable and welcoming; others, cold and cheerless.

Stories about bad billets abounded:

"My landlady was so mean," said one teenage Park worker. "She complained about me reading in bed and using the electricity . . . I disregarded her comments. One night the light went off—she had switched off the mains!"

"My accommodation was with the local undertaker," grumbled another. "His quaint little wife promised me for the bottom of my drawer some of the lace doilies which were used to cover the faces of the corpses. I didn't take up the offer."

"My room was above the hotel bar and smelled strongly

of beer," complained yet another. "Ice came out the taps and there was no heating whatsoever. . . ."

Jane knew she was luckier than some. The family she billeted with was kind. But their lifestyle completely differed from anything the debutante had known. Besides the noise, the house sat right next to the brick factory with its smoke-belching chimneys. "It really was disgusting," said Jane. So was the toilet. Located outside in the garden, it used torn-up newspaper for tissue. The debutante had to move!

Rather than wait for the billeting office to find her an alternative place to live, Jane took matters into her own hands. A friend of her father's, Sir Reginald Bonsor, lived in a country manor eight miles from Bletchley. Most of his servants had left for the military, so he had plenty of spare rooms. Best of all, the billeting officer hadn't knocked on his stately front door yet. Jane beat him to it. Would Sir Reginald take her in?

He did, along with six other young women working at the Park.

Jane's new bedroom was roomy and sunlit, and overlooked the rose garden. An orchard and kitchen garden guaranteed ample fruits and vegetables, and a grand piano in the ballroom ensured entertainment. Sometimes Lady Bonsor even held dinner parties. She asked soldiers on leave to dine with the family, then invited Jane and the other girls to join them. The eighteen-year-old thoroughly enjoyed these events. It felt wonderful to put on a pretty dress, laugh, and chat. A few times they'd even put records on the wind-up gramophone and danced. At those times, briefly, she forgot about Hut 6 and her Typex machine and the dreadful war.

Mavis, billeted with the local grocer in rooms above the store, had a different experience. "I looked after the children. I babysat. I helped on the farm. I did my own washing," she remembered. And all this after wrestling with Enigma ciphers for eight hours! Of course, the family she lived with knew nothing about her work at Bletchley Park. Mavis hadn't whispered a word. And the family asked no questions. But did they suspect something?

The landlady knew Mavis worked hard. As a treat, she insisted on bringing a cup of tea to the teenager's bedroom every morning.

One day, after setting the steaming cup on the bedside table, she told Mavis she would be gone for a while. But not to worry, she said, "My aunt will be coming to look after you."

Mavis asked if she was going on vacation.

"Actually, I'm having a baby," the landlady replied.

Mavis felt awful. The landlady shouldn't have been waiting on *her*. She should have been waiting on the *landlady*. Why hadn't she said anything?

The landlady laughed, then said slyly, "You know, you're not the only one who can keep a secret."

BLITZ!

It began around four p.m. on September 7, 1940. Londoners gradually became aware of a distant muffled roar like thunder that grew louder and louder. Suddenly, the sky grew dark as 348 German planes began dropping high explosive bombs and incendiary devices on the city. Flames billowed. Buildings collapsed. Terrified citizens streamed toward air raid shelters as wave after wave of enemy aircraft flew overhead. It was the start of an intense Nazi bombing campaign known as the Blitz after the German word *blitzkrieg* (lightning war). In just a few hours, 430 people were killed and 1,600 injured.

The British called it "Black Saturday."

A bomb-damaged street in London.

England's new prime minister, Winston Churchill, called it "cruel [and] wanton."

Black Saturday would be just the beginning. For the next fifty-seven straight nights, German bombers pounded London, dropping an incredible nineteen thousand tons of bombs on the city. In November, they expanded the Blitz to raid other British cities—Liverpool, Birmingham, Manchester. They pummeled port cities in Wales, Scotland, and Northern Ireland—all with the goal of bringing the British to their knees and forcing them to surrender.

A London family loses everything but their lives after a German bombing.

A view of London lit by flames during an air raid.

While bombs scream overhead, Londoners settle down beneath the streets in the safety of the city's Underground (subway tunnels).

* * *

In Hut 6, Jane and the others worked with a new and terrible urgency. The Luftwaffe used Enigma (code-named the Brown Enigma by Bletchley Park) to direct its bombers to their London targets. Around midday every day, it named the targets for that night's raid.

Every day, the boffins scrambled to break into Brown Enigma's settings. Knowing German targets in advance meant saving British lives. Hunched over the intercepts, their minds roiled with cribs and wheel settings and five-letter groups. Occasionally, one of them glanced up at the clock on the wall. How long had they been working? Was there still enough time to warn people?

Some days, the boffins excitedly shouted, "Got it!"

Then Jane and the others in the Decoding Room hurried to their Typex machines. The supervisor handed around the intercepts, and gave out the settings. Jane shifted wheels, adjusted plugs, and clicked the machine's clogs. Then she was off, fingers flying.

The names of German targets spooled out the machine's top:

The London Port

The Avonmouth aircraft factories

Buckingham Palace

A rare photo of Hut 6's Decoding Room. After 1941, photographs of the Park were largely forbidden.

The names of these targets were sent straight to London. Then all of Hut 6 waited. Had there been enough time to evacuate? Could authorities get citizens safely into air raid shelters? Was the British Royal Air Force (RAF) waiting in ambush for the German bombers when they arrived? For security reasons, higher-ups never told them if their efforts had succeeded.

Still, Jane never doubted the importance of her work. She'd been home on leave and seen the effects of the bombings—the homes turned to dust, the huge craters where schools and hospitals once stood, the boarded-up windows and rubble-filled streets. But that was not the worst of it. Forty-three thousand British men, women, and children would lose their lives during the eight months of the Blitz. That number staggered Jane. And it made those times when the Brown Enigma could not be broken unbearably painful.

Sadly, there were many of those times.

For four straight days in November, Hut 6 failed to unravel Brown Enigma's settings. One of those days was November 14. Around dinnertime, remembered one staff member, "all these German bombers started screaming over [Bletchley Park] so we knew someone was being blown up and we hadn't been able to alert them."

A morgue-like silence fell over the hut.

That night the town of Coventry was bombed to rubble. Six hundred people died.

The Cathedral in Coventry, dating from the fourteenth century, is reduced to little more than rubble and ash by Nazi aircraft.

At the Withernsea Y Station, Patricia turned the dial of her wireless radio. Suddenly, she heard a whooshing sound. It was a warming-up signal. Patricia stopped moving her dial, and waited.

Moments later, a German voice came through Patricia's headphones. It was a Nazi soldier and he spoke in perfect English. "I know you British are listening. Can you hear me?" His tone sounded cheerful. "Would you like me to drop a bomb on you? Listen—wheee!—boomp!" He chuckled into his radio's microphone.

Patricia jumped back, startled. Other Y station listeners had heard these messages. They even had a name for them—"ghost voices." But Patricia had never heard one, until now. It was her first ghost voice. It would not be her last.

If You Were a Code and Cipher Cracker: Clues

It's not easy to break a cipher. But there are five clues that will help you do so. These clues are found in the way words are spelled, and in the number of times certain letters are usually used. These five clues are:

Clue #1: Frequency—How often do letters appear? The letter E, for example, is the most ordinary letter in the English language. In almost every page of printed written words, the letter E appears more often than any other letter. Here are the ten most often used letters in English, in order of frequency:

ETAONRISHD

Clue #2: "Double" letters—These are letters used in pairs, as in the words ROLL, MEET, TOOL, CLASS. In English, these letters are most often doubled:

LL EE SS OO TT

Clue #3: Combinations of two different letters that often appear together—The combination TH, for example, appears in such words as: THAT, THE, THIS, THING, PATH. Two-letter combinations that appear most often in English are, in the order of their frequency:

TH HE AN RE ER IN

Clue #4: Combinations of three letters that appear together. The combination THE, for example, is a word in itself. But it also appears in many other words, such as OTHER, FATHER, TOGETHER. The combination ING appears in lots of words, too, such as SING, GOING, WALKING. Three-letter combinations that appear most often in English are, in order of their frequency:

THE ING AND ION ENT

Clue #5: One letter standing alone. In English, that will almost certainly be I or A. That is why many cryptographers will first encipher a message, and then break it up into groups of five letters each, instead of writing it in separate words. You will see why this makes it more difficult to decipher a message if you break up the sentence TEN BATTALIONS HEADED WEST into groups of five letters each, running words together or breaking them in the middle if necessary. That sentence now looks like this: TENBA TTALI ONSHE ADEDW ESTAX. The two letters at the end—A and X—are called **nulls**. They've been added to make the last "word" five letters long. Nulls have no secret meaning, but they do make deciphering the message even harder.

Of course, in a very short message, the five clues listed above might not help break a cipher. There's simply not enough to work with. The same can be said for messages full of technical terms and other unfamiliar words. In that case, the usual ways in which words and letters are used is often disrupted. And even though E is the most frequently used letter in the English language, it is possible to write a message with no E's at all, like: SHIP SAILS TONIGHT. If that sentence were enciphered, you'd have trouble breaking in, because your most important clue would give you no help at all.

In your next lesson, we will use these clues—and all you've learned about them—to start deciphering.

1941

CIPHERS, SPIES, AND A
MYSTERIOUS SUMMONS

8

A MYSTERIOUS SUMMONS

The letter arrived in an ordinary brown envelope. It did not have a return address. And inside there was just a single piece of paper that read:

> You are to report to Station X at
> Bletchley Park, Buckinghamshire
> in four days time . . . That is all you
> need to know.
>
> Signed
> Commander Travis

Eighteen-year-old Sarah Norton was puzzled. Who was this "Commander Travis," and what in the world was "Station X"? Her always-fertile imagination raced. Would she be going down into coal mines, or servicing fighter planes on wintry airfields?

In truth, she knew nothing about coal mines or fighter planes. The daughter of the 6th Lord Grantley lived a charmed life of horseback riding, boarding school, and country manors. Her beloved godfather, the 1st Earl Mountbatten of Burma, was related to the royal family. Her grandmother was Queen Elizabeth's best friend.

Sarah reread the letter, and a more pressing question sprang to mind: "What on earth do you [pack] when you have no idea what the job is?"

The teenager spent the next three days digging around in her closet. Eventually, she filled her suitcase with what she considered the bare essentials—five daytime outfits, an evening gown with matching shoes, lipstick, and, most importantly, her teddy bear. She also dragged along a heavy windup gramophone and dozens of records. They *were* a bit of a burden, but one couldn't go without music, could one?

On the fourth day, as summoned, she arrived at Bletchley Station. No one was there to meet her . . . or carry her luggage.

King George VI.

A glimpse into Sarah's privileged childhood. Here she sits (far right) with her mother and brother, as well as her well-connected godmother, Edwina Mountbatten (in the hat) at a beach in France.

Queen Elizabeth (middle), wife of King George VI and dear friend to Sarah's grandmother, visits female factory workers, c. 1941.

Balancing bags, records, and bear, she staggered up a narrow path and headed toward what was obviously Bletchley Park. The mansion came into view. "It is grotesque! A Victorian monstrosity," she opined to the officer who waited at the gate. After dumping her luggage in the house's main hall, she followed him up to Commander Travis's office.

"I hear you speak German," he said without introductions.

Sarah was startled. Two years earlier, while still in school, her parents had sent her to Munich for six months to broaden her horizons and learn the language. Hitler was

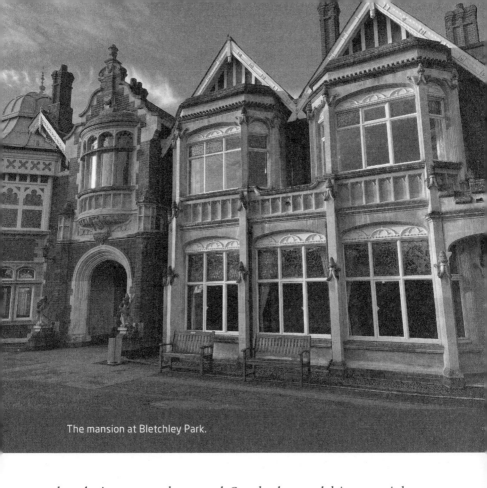
The mansion at Bletchley Park.

already in power then, and Sarah detested him on sight. She'd refused to raise her arm in salute when the Führer appeared, and had taken to visiting the Charlton Tea Room, a place Hitler frequented. Choosing a table as close to him as possible, Sarah would stare at him with obvious distaste. Too bad he never seemed to notice her. Still, it had given the teenager vicarious pleasure.

Did Commander Travis know all this?

Sarah admitted that she *did* speak German.

And Commander Travis launched into a vague talk about the work being done at Bletchley. "Its primary purpose," he said, "[is] to break the German machine codes." But he refused to elaborate further. What he did make crystal clear, however, was that secrecy was of the utmost importance. Then he pushed a document toward her—the Official Secrets Act.

Sarah signed it. Minutes later, she left his office still not knowing what she'd be doing at the Park. Instead, she was escorted to Hut 4, part of the German Naval Section. A long, green-painted shack, Hut 4 squatted next to the mansion like a frog. Sarah didn't know it yet, but all decrypts pertaining to the Kriegsmarine ended up here after first being deciphered in Hut 8.

Sarah was led to the Index Room. Here, around a tall table, perched several young women on high stools. They bent over long box files, raking through stacks of enemy messages and making notes on index cards. Finally, Sarah learned what her job would be: Indexer.

All decrypts—after being translated into English—arrived in the Index Room. The Indexer's job was to scrutinize each one for bits of useful intelligence. She picked out key words like the name of a ship, or the captain who sent it. She noted coordinates, code names, weapons, units, places, and scientific names. One of the Indexers even had the tedious job of making a note every time Bletchley Park learned that a German submarine (or "U-boat") had fired a torpedo. By keeping track, higher-ups could tell how many of these underwater weapons each enemy submarine had left. And torpedo stocks were just *one* of the thousands of details that were regularly recorded. Nothing was too small, or too trivial.

The Indexer wrote all this information on index cards. Any time a new word came up—for example, an officer's name—she would create a reference for it. Then this information was collated and filed in a huge card index already containing hundreds of thousands of names, units, postings, supply requisitions, details of promotions, court martials, and leaves of absence. Bletchley Park kept everything so it would know everything. Even something as seemingly trivial as the transfer of a Luftwaffe lieutenant could tip off British intelligence agents to an impending attack. Higher-ups considered the index vitally important.

Sarah, of course, didn't know any of this yet. On this chilly, early spring morning, she glanced around her new workplace, then pulled up the collar of her thick, Scottish-wool cardigan. Despite the ancient stove in the corner, the room remained cold. That was because the stove let out more

BERGEN
1945
3.1.4.

COMO LAKE
V.1 components made in

Kolding

Nordisk

NORWEG
ROOKET
omket

JAATTAN
1945
7.2.

BUCHENWA
Frenc

HEIDELF
S.S. train
Rocket expos
Battle Sch
1944
9 Aug. 44. Rocke
21.8.44. Rocke
6.11.44. 40%
29/12/44. Menh
20/4/45 Lehr
staalhoo

VARRELT
1944
29.10. 8/KG
1945 2 good
7.1.

AMSTERDAM
Warsitzwerke at — made in
Warsitzwerke at — ar
shortly close down
in part of former

F.P.N. 162427-M(?)P(?) is at
Night A 5-6/3/45 2 trains with V.1s
2 HAARLEM

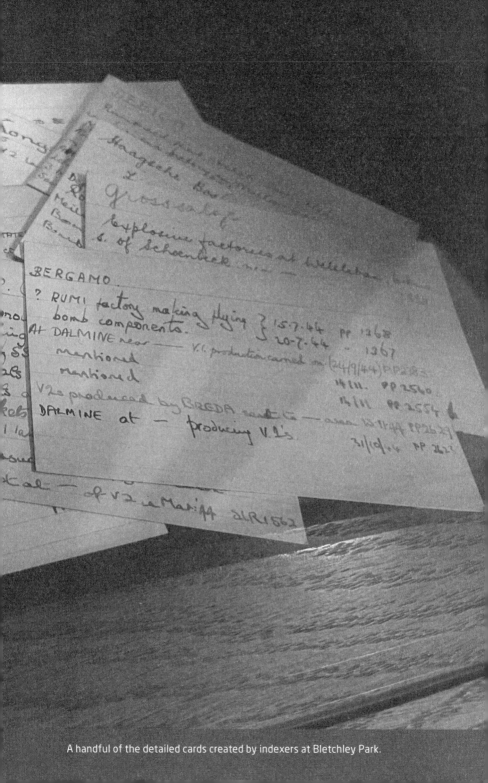

A handful of the detailed cards created by indexers at Bletchley Park.

Just a minuscule portion of the vast card index currently on display at the Bletchley Park Trust Archives Museum.

smoke than heat. The ventilation was awful due to the sand-bags and brick walls built around the hut to protect it in case of an air raid, so the room smelled sooty. Even with the windows open, Sarah would soon learn, no breeze or natural light made its way into the room.

Sitting down at the table, she decided to keep her hat and gloves on.

Her new boss, a tall, thin, gloomy-looking officer named Commander Crawford, pushed a stack of index cards and a box of colored pencils toward her. Topics were cataloged by colors and abbreviations, he told her. He explained the system.

It was complex and hard to grasp. Was there a chart Sarah could refer to?

Absolutely not. The system was classified information. Officials couldn't risk writing it down. Sarah would have to learn as she went.

The teenager took a decrypt from the cardboard box in the middle of the table. It had thin strips of paper tape stuck onto it. Later, she would learn that these were the strips from the Typex machines. But this day, she could only stare at it, feeling overwhelmed. Where to start? The others didn't look up from their work. Obviously, Sarah was on her own.

Those first days on the job were difficult ones. She hunched over the decrypts, looking up now and then to blot her cold, dripping nose with one of her lace handkerchiefs. What did the letters LW stand for again? Luftwaffe or leber-wurst (liver sausage)? What color was used to record U-boat locations? Learning *how* to do the job was going to take time.

But it took Sarah less than twenty-four hours to real-ize *what* she was doing. "I was cross-referencing Top Secret material, information that very few others . . . were allowed to see, let alone know about." She had no idea where the information came from, and all the while she worked in the Index Room, she never once heard the word "Enigma." Still, she knew she was privy to something extraordinary. Sarah Norton, daughter of the 6th Lord Grantley, knew national secrets!

X-3

In Cottage 3, Mavis Lever—alone on the night shift—sat hunched over her desk. She could see her breath, and the windows, covered with blackout curtains, shook with each gust of chilly March wind. Mavis was still working on the Italian Naval Enigma. Over the past months she'd come to think of them as word games. Some days she hadn't been able to break into the cipher no matter how she tried. Other days, however, an Italian phrase would come swimming out of the rows of gibberish. Then she handed a worked-out message to Dilly.

Because she didn't know Italian, she always had to ask what they said. So far they'd all been routine—weather bulletins, or messages that read "nothing to report."

It didn't matter, Dilly insisted. The content of those messages wasn't important. What was vital was actually breaking into that day's setting. Key broken, the Typex operators could set their machines and run through the rest of the intercepts. Of course, Mavis would never learn what the rest of those intercepts revealed. The Park's "need to know" policy prohibited that.

This night, the Cottage's wire baskets overflowed with intercepts. Traffic analysis had determined they were from the Italian Naval Command in Rome. Mavis figured they were "dummy messages." The enemy often sent endless streams of messages in hopes that the British (who they knew were listening) wouldn't notice when they sent something important. Mavis reached into the basket. It was a short one, just a few lines. She steeled herself. The short ones were always the hardest to decipher because there was so little to work with.

Her pencil scratched across paper. Chopped logic. Could the Y in the cipher text stand for E? Maybe. At least it gave her a start. Her guess yielded up two or three more potential letters within the message. And then . . .

The cipher text clicked into place. Even with her limited Italian, Mavis could make it out:

TODAY 25 MARCH IS X-3

The teenager immediately grasped its meaning. The Italian Navy was going to do something big in three days' time. But what?

Those in the Cottage worked around the clock trying to answer that question. Each of the following three days had different Enigma settings, meaning each message had to be broken separately. For the next three days, they hardly ate, and just grabbed snatches of sleep. Dilly was so focused on the incoming intercepts that he tried to stuff a cheese sandwich instead of his tobacco into his pipe. Mavis bit her fingernails down to the quick. She worked shift after shift, never leaving the Cottage. When the wire basket grew empty, she paced the cottage floor, listening anxiously for the roar of the motorcycle dispatch riders bringing the newly intercepted messages. She and the others pounced on them the minute they arrived.

But time was slipping away. X-3 became X-2. X-2 became X-1. What vital information was the cipher protecting?

Then a long message came in. All of them leaped at it, each taking a section back to their desks. Now the only sound in the Cottage was pencils tapping and murmuring voices. Day turned to night. Letter by letter, word by word, they broke into the cipher.

Dilly translated the decrypted lines from Italian to English.

Battle plans. And it was all there. In detail, Italian Naval Command had laid out their intentions to attack British troop convoys sailing from Egypt to Greece. The plan specified times and places, as well as the number of cruisers and submarines.

They'd done it!

"It was eleven o'clock at night, and it was pouring rain when I rushed, ran, absolutely tore down to take it to Intelligence," said Mavis.

But would it arrive in time to save British sailors?

Later that week, on a well-deserved day off, Mavis went to the movie theater. As she sat in the flickering darkness, a newsreel came on-screen. These short films about current events often touched on happenings in the war. And this one, titled "After the Battle," was no exception. The black-and-white film showed grinning British sailors, ships, and torpedoes. A chipper announcer narrated:

With our Navy's brilliant victory over the Italian Fleet in the Mediterranean at Cape Matapan, let us watch as our victorious ships return to [Egypt]. Our sailors did grand work in the battle. They sent [five ships] to the bottom of the ocean . . . and our Navy lost not a man, not a ship and not even a square inch of paint!

A scene of nighttime action as British warships bombard Italian battleships at the Cape of Matapan.

The Italian naval fleet was virtually destroyed, and would hardly be heard from again during the war. Now the newsreel camera panned over the deck of the HMS *Warsprite*, where a tall officer in dress uniform stood smiling. Said the announcer:

Ladies and gentlemen, we take the utmost pride in Presenting . . . that victor of Cape Matapan, [Commander-in-Chief of the Royal Navy's Mediterranean Fleet] Admiral Sir Andrew Cunningham!

The moviegoers cheered. In this bleak spring of 1941—as German planes pummeled London and German U-boats torpedoed English ships in the North Sea—British citizens badly needed a morale-boosting victory. Admiral Cunningham had given it to them.

But not, Mavis knew, without the help of the Cottage.

Secretly, she glowed with pride.

10

BY LEAPS AND BOUNDS AND TEA AND TOAST

Bletchley Park grew fast. When Jane and Mavis arrived, just a few hundred people worked there. By the time Sarah walked through the gate a year later, fourteen hundred people—four hundred men and one thousand women (most of them under the age of twenty-one)—typed, filed, translated languages, and pitted their minds against the Enigma cipher. Additionally, there were cleaners, gardeners, and maintenance people. And there was the Transport Section, many of them members of the women's branch of the army, called the Auxiliary Territorial Service, or ATS. They drove the buses that took workers to and from their billets, and undertook special duties such as delivering dispatches to the Admiralty in London or chauffeuring VIPs.

All these people required feeding. At the start, the mansion's dining room had been big enough. But in 1941, a new hut was built, and it became the Park's canteen. Now, during their breaks, Jane and Mavis wandered over for a bowl of soup or plate of milk pudding.

But Sarah steered clear of the place. The food, she claimed, was "indescribably bad." She understood the difficulty of cooking around the clock for hundreds of people, especially with wartime rationing. Still, the canteen "outshone any sleazy restaurant in producing sludge," she declared. The place, smelling as it did of watery cabbage and stale fat, made her queasy.

However, she did brave a meal one night at the canteen, only to be served a cockroach with her meat. Disgusted, she pushed back from the table, intending to return it.

"What a waste!" piped up the girl sitting next to her. "I'll eat round it." And she snatched Sarah's plate away and gobbled down everything but the bug.

Sarah was horrified.

She was also hungry.

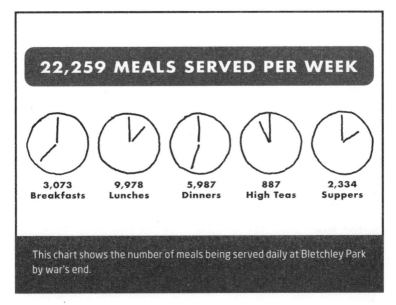

22,259 MEALS SERVED PER WEEK

3,073
Breakfasts

9,978
Lunches

5,987
Dinners

887
High Teas

2,334
Suppers

This chart shows the number of meals being served daily at Bletchley Park by war's end.

So who could blame her for smuggling an electric cooker ring into the Index Room?

She hid it in the closet, where—because of the hut's weird architectural features—there was an electrical outlet. Whenever Commander Crawford wasn't around, she and the others staved off hunger by using the cooker ring to brew tea or heat up a can of baked beans.

One evening, Sarah arrived for the late shift with a loaf of bread. Around midnight, her stomach growled. Time for tea and toast!

She and her friend Jean were dangling slices of bread over the glowing cooking ring when Crawford burst into the room.

Jean managed to shut the closet door just as Crawford shouted, "I smell toast!" He looked around for the offending snack.

Planting an innocent look on her face, Jean piped up. The smell was coming from her, she explained. "I always smell of toast."

Crawford sputtered in disbelief. He knew the girls were up to something. But he didn't see anything out of place. Ordering them back to work, he stomped out of the room.

The moment the door closed behind him, the girls burst into laughter. Sarah and Jean went back to making toast.

Despite the hijinks, Sarah took her job seriously. In the months since her arrival, she'd not only become proficient at the cataloging system but also had become an expert on the information found on those thousands of index cards (by war's end there would be millions, enough to fill three large rooms). If asked what she knew about a particular German warship or commander, she could quickly pull out the facts from the mountains of material. "Odd pieces of information seemed to stick in my brain, making it quicker to find the correct card," she later said.

Good thing, too, because almost daily someone from "the watch" would appear at the Index Room's windowed hatch.

The watch was where decrypted messages were analyzed and interpreted. But the watch keepers often couldn't figure out what a message meant without additional information. And so one of them would walk across the hall to speak with an indexer.

For example, he might show her a decrypt that read:

> **140,000 Liters GA3 to 50 41 30 N—03 04 30 E by 2100**

Could Sarah help? Did she have any cards about "GA3," or "50 41 30 N-03 04 30 E"?

Indeed, she did. A card titled "GA3" indicated this was a high-grade fuel. Another card titled "50 41 30 N-03 04 30 E" showed these as coordinates for the Saint-Nazaire submarine base in France. This card also noted that the Nazis had been engaged in construction of the base for the last ninety-five days.

But Sarah told the watch keeper even more. Because of meticulous cross-referencing, she knew that a message to the Kriegsmarine high command had been decrypted just eighteen hours earlier. This decrypt reported that the submarine base was now operational. And that wasn't all. Another message decrypted just three hours ago reported three U-boats en route to that same base.

In mere minutes, Sarah had put together bits and pieces of information that gave the watch keeper's decrypt a fuller meaning. What did he do with the information? Sarah would never find out. But most of the time, he rushed off smiling and shouting thanks.

11

A VISIT FROM ADMIRAL CUNNINGHAM

One morning in April, Dilly Knox made an announcement: a special guest was on his way to meet the Cottage staff—Admiral Sir Andrew Cunningham!

Mavis and the others grew flustered. The admiral was coming *now*? They scurried around picking up papers and emptying trash cans. What about refreshments? They couldn't possibly offer the "Hero of Matapan" a weak cup of tea and cabbage soup. Mavis and a colleague rushed to the Eight Bells pub just outside the Park to buy some wine. They got back in time to smooth their hair before lining up outside the Cottage. Admiral Cunningham in his gold-braided uniform shook hands down the line.

"We all thought him very handsome and dashing," said Mavis, "especially when he drank a toast to [us] for having put the Italian Navy out of action for the rest of the war."

The girls tried to act serious. But they could feel laughter rising like bubbles. Yes, they'd broken an important cipher, but they were still so young. Just teenagers. Wouldn't it be funny to play a trick on the admiral? Conveniently, the cottage walls had just been whitewashed, and the paint was still wet.

"We thought it would be jolly funny if we got him to lean against the wet white wash in his lovely dark uniform," said Mavis.

Somehow, they maneuvered him to brush against the wall.

When he left, they could barely stifle their giggles. From the back end, the "Hero of Matapan" looked a bit like a skunk.

12

FIND THE *BISMARCK*

Bismarck cruised the North Atlantic like a shark. The most formidable ship ever built, and the largest, *Bismarck* was the German Navy's pride. Its mission was to sink British convoys returning from the United States with oil, food, and other desperately needed war supplies. By severing the supply line between England and the United States, Hitler hoped to starve the British into submission. *Bismarck* posed the biggest threat to British shipping in the North Atlantic.

But on May 24, in the waters between Greenland and Iceland, *Bismarck* encountered the battle cruiser HMS *Hood*, the flagship of the Royal Navy. For four thundering minutes the two vessels pounded at each other. Shells screamed

The *Bismarck*.

overhead. Water exploded. Then one of *Bismarck*'s shells ripped through *Hood*'s deck, piercing its ammunition storage and causing a huge explosion. *Hood* broke in half and sank beneath the waves. All but two of its crew members sank with it.

Bismarck, however, had not escaped unscathed. One of *Hood*'s shells had ruptured an oil tank. The mighty battleship was leaking fuel and taking on seawater. It needed repair. *Bismarck*'s captain turned the ship toward port.

But which port?

Top brass at the Admiralty guessed *Bismarck* was headed for Norway and ordered the Royal Navy fleet to go after it. They were determined to hunt the ship down and sink it.

Meanwhile, at Bletchley Park, workers in Hut 8—German Naval Section—grappled with *Bismarck*'s radio signals. They couldn't decipher them. But it was clear the ship was communicating with radio operators in Paris. If this was the case, the only logical port to repair the ship was at Brest.

Intelligence officers from Hut 4 telephoned the Admiralty with this information. But officers there refused to listen. They believed their original assumption was correct. The Royal Fleet chugged on toward Norway.

In Hut 6, Jane Hughes came on shift. Settling in front of her Typex, she adjusted its settings and began typing. She punched the keys. Out spewed the now-familiar five-letter blocks of German. One word caught her eye: Brest.

Her typing slowed. Around her, others still clacked away. But Jane leaned in closer to read the decrypts.

The first was from a Luftwaffe general. He'd sent an enciphered message asking for the whereabouts of *Bismarck* because his son was on board.

The return messages told him: *Bismarck* and his son were headed for Brest.

Jane leaped to her feet. Everyone knew the Royal Navy was searching for *Bismarck*. Newspapers and radio programs had been filled with reports about the battle and the sinking of

HMS *Hood*. She shouted for Keith Batey, one of the cryptographers, to come take a look.

Batey, too, recognized the importance of the decrypts. He rushed them to Hut 3's intelligence agents, who immediately sent out a top secret message to the Admiralty: "INFORMATION RECEIVED GRADED A-1 . . . BISMARCK IS HEADED FOR WEST COAST OF FRANCE."

A-1 was the highest grade Bletchley Park could give its intelligence. It meant there was absolutely no doubt.

This time the Admiralty listened.

Hours later, through storm-tossed waves, British warships and planes found the wounded *Bismarck*. They attacked. The battleship could do little to save itself. Within hours it sank, taking twenty-three hundred men to the ocean's bottom.

The news demoralized German citizens. Even Hitler, noted one senior Reich official, "is melancholy beyond words." But in Britain, people rejoiced. The mighty symbol of Nazi naval strength had been scuttled.

Jane, however, didn't feel jubilant. She couldn't stop thinking about the men who'd drowned. Yes, they were the enemy. But they were also someone's husband, father, or brother.

Mavis Lever didn't rejoice either. She knew the intelligence had come from Bletchley Park even if she didn't know how.

Some did survive the sinking of the *Bismarck*. Here German sailors are hauled aboard a British warship.

And she couldn't stop thinking about it. "How awful it was that one's breaking of a cipher could send so many people to the bottom." She wrestled with these feelings. And eventually, she stiffened her resolve. "This is war," she reminded herself, "and this is the way we have to play it. If we think about it too much we will never be able to cope."

13

THE GEESE THAT NEVER CACKLE

In September, Prime Minister Winston Churchill visited Bletchley Park. He toured several huts, including Hut 6, where he watched Jane give a demonstration of the Typex machine. Gordon Welchman, a mathematician in charge of Hut 6, explained the complexity of the Enigma machine to the prime minister. Churchill listened closely, his appreciation and respect for the Park's work growing.

When it came time for him to leave, the prime minister hesitated.

It was a shift change, and the Park bustled with people. Climbing onto some building rubble, Churchill spontaneously addressed the workers. Sarah, who'd been hurrying to

Prime Minister Winston Churchill preparing to give a radio address.

Hut 4, stopped. So did Mavis, who had been en route to the Cottage. Jane stepped out of Hut 6.

Churchill stood there a moment as a cold wind ruffled his wispy gray hair. He thrust his hand into the vest pocket of his pinstriped suit. "You all look very innocent; one would not think you would know anything secret!" he finally said. "But I know better. You're my geese who lay the golden eggs—and never cackle."

His words brought a loud cheer from the staff. Then Churchill gave a wave, hopped down, and got into his car. Ever after, he would call the intelligence received from the Park his "eggs." And he would insist on having a few of these "eggs" brought to his office at 10 Downing Street every morning. These decrypts, fresh from Bletchley Park, came in a beige-colored lockbox and were hand delivered by a secret agent known only as "C." Churchill alone could open the box with a key he kept on his key ring.

The secrets contained in the decrypts delighted the prime minister. He took real pleasure in vexing top military brass by telling them snippets of information they'd not yet heard. What was Churchill's source? "Boniface," he would reply. It was his code word for Bletchley Park.

Encouraged by Churchill's embrace of the work being done

at the Park, a handful of cryptanalysts wrote to him a month after his visit. They begged him for more staff. "We think you ought to know," they wrote, "that work is being held up, and in some cases not being done at all, principally because we cannot get sufficient staff to deal with it." They needed clerks and typists, they explained. They needed Typex operators and indexers. They needed Wrens and WAAFs (members of the Women's Auxiliary Air Force). In short, they needed more female personnel to help gather those golden "eggs."

After reading this letter, Churchill pulled out a red sticker printed with the words "Action This Day" and stuck it to the top of the letter. Then he sent an urgent memorandum to his chief of staff. "Make sure they have all they want on extreme priority and report to me that this has been done," he ordered. From here on out, Bletchley Park would get whatever resources it needed.

14

THE SPY ENIGMA

S pring turned to summer, and those in the Cottage had less and less to do. Admiral Cunningham's visit was practically the last time Mavis would hear of the Italian fleet. Its reduced activity meant fewer Enigma messages. By July, the Cottage's wire baskets held just a handful of intercepts. It was time, Park officials decided, for the Cottage to tackle a new problem: the Abwehr Enigma.

Abwehr was the name of Germany's intelligence-gathering organization. Its secret agents used an Enigma machine when communicating. But unlike other Enigma machines, with their standard three rotors, the Abwehr Enigma (Dilly Knox called it the "Spy Enigma") had four. To make things more complicated, the Spy Enigma's rotors turned more often

The German Abwehr Enigma. Note the four rotors at the top.

and with no predictable pattern. Sometimes, all four rotors even turned over at the same time. The Nazi spy network believed this made their enigma machine ciphers impossible to crack. And many people at Bletchley Park thought so, too. In fact, cryptographers in Hut 6 had unsuccessfully wrestled with it for months. They understood the vital importance of Abwehr intercepts. Imagine all that top secret information gathered by Nazi spies just waiting to be read. But unable to crack them, the Park's cryptographers had been forced to file them away.

Now the Spy Enigma landed in the Cottage's lap. Dilly Knox was determined to crack it. Disregarding the Park's secrecy policy, he called his female team of cryptographers together and explained what they were up against. Mavis listened carefully.

It had begun back in 1940, he told them, when Hitler plotted a land invasion of England. In advance of this invasion, he'd secreted a cadre of Nazi spies into the country. But British Secret Intelligence agents (MI5) had immediately caught most of them. These captured spies had been given a choice: face the firing squad or do exactly as an MI5 agent ordered. Most had chosen the second option. Now they were double agents, pretending to act as spies for Germany while actually working on behalf of England. Through these double agents, MI5 had been feeding the Nazis false information meant to fool them. MI5 called this operation the "Double Cross System."

What did all this have to do with the Spy Enigma?

The double agents sent their false information to Nazi controllers in Paris, Lisbon, and Madrid. These controllers analyzed everything received. If they believed the information was credible, they forwarded it on to Berlin . . . using the Abwehr Enigma machine. The only way to know for sure if the Nazis believed what the British were feeding them was to read these messages. The Cottage *had* to break in.

Mavis got to work. Day after day she pitted her brains against the Abwehr Enigma. But the work wasn't anything like that of breaking into the Italian Navy's settings. While

An Abwehr radio station in Hamburg, Germany. Inside, Nazi controllers analyzed every scrap of information sent to them by the Nazi agents across the world.

that had been excruciating, it had also been exciting and ultimately satisfying. Wrestling with the Abwehr Enigma, however, was an endless slog of trying one thing, then another, and another. Her frustration mounted. So did her anxiety. Even in her off-hours, her thoughts churned like rotor turns.

So did Dilly's. He spent day and night in the Cottage, fired by endless cups of black coffee and flashes of inspiration. Like Mavis, it was the rotor turns that obsessed him. How many turnovers did each wheel have? If he could find a way to discover how and when the wheels turned over, might he then learn how the letters on the wheel related to those turnovers?

One afternoon he pulled out his favorite book, Lewis Carroll's *Sylvie and Bruno*. He loved the author's strange logic and wordplay—so like cryptographic puzzle solving. He read a passage aloud to his team:

> *In science . . . in fact in most things, it is usually best to begin at the beginning. In some things, of course, it's better to begin at the end. For instance, if you wanted to paint a dog green, it might be better to begin with the tail, as it doesn't bite the end.*

Mavis pondered the passage. What was Dilly getting at?

Didn't they see? "Everything that has a middle has also a beginning and an end!" he exclaimed.

After one especially long night in the Cottage, Dilly met Mavis and another cryptographer, Margaret Rock, at the Cottage door. He was beside himself with excitement. "If two cows are crossing the road," he said "there must be a point where there is only one and that's what we must find."

Mavis and Margaret traded looks.

"Lobsters!" shouted Dilly.

Neither grasped a word of it. But they knew when Dilly fired off ideas it was best to stay quiet. Eventually, he would get around to making sense.

And he did. "Lobsters" was his word for when all four rotors of the Abwehr Enigma machine turned over at the same time. A much longer stream of text often followed these lobsters without any further rotor turns. *This* was the place where the machine was vulnerable, he told them.

It was time to go on a lobster hunt. If they could track down the lobsters, he believed they could get into the settings.

Mavis and Margaret began hunting, systematically looking for messages where his idea would work.

Then one night, after weeks of working day and night, Dilly collapsed. Unknown to his team, he'd been battling stomach cancer. Now, too weak to return to the Cottage, he continued to work from home. Margaret Rock went with him. Incredibly, Mavis took charge of the Cottage. She'd just turned twenty.

A few days later, Mavis found a "very fine lobster." This allowed Dilly to work out the turnover patterns for one of the wheels.

December frosts had already hardened the Park's lake before Mavis finally broke into a message between Abwehr agents in Berlin and Belgrade, Yugoslavia (modern-day Serbia). It was strange how everything fell into place, letters spiraling and chaining. Suddenly, out of the gibberish came blocks of German text.

Mavis felt both elated and exhausted. When it came to deciphering, she said, "It was serendipity that counted. And it seemed to me that there was a good chance of finding lobsters and sometimes it worked, and sometimes it didn't, and this time it did."

From this point on, Bletchley Park was reading almost all the messages between German intelligence agents.

And MI5 knew with certainty that the Germans believed all the fake information they were being fed.

That night, after finally breaking into the Spy Enigma, Mavis headed back to her billet. Did she note the date of her breakthrough?

It was December 7, 1941.

PEARL HARBOR

Prime Minister Winston Churchill was having dinner when he heard the news. A butler brought a portable radio into the dining room for him to listen to the British Broadcasting Home Service. The Japanese had attacked an American naval base in Pearl Harbor, Hawaii.

An American warship after Imperial Japan's attack on Pearl Harbor.

Churchill telephoned President Franklin Roosevelt. "Mr. President, what's this with Japan?" he asked.

Roosevelt confirmed it was true. "We're all in the same boat now," he added.

To Churchill, this meant one thing above all: victory. Britain would no longer be fighting Germany alone. Finally, the United States would enter the war.

President Franklin D. Roosevelt (left) and Prime Minister Winston Churchill (right), partners and leaders in a war against the Axis powers.

On December 8, the United States declared war on Japan.

That same day, Britain also declared war on Japan.

Three days later, on December 11, because of the military pact they'd made with Japan, both Germany and Italy declared war on the United States.

This prompted the US to declare war on them just hours later.

The world was now torn in two. There were the Allied forces headed by the United States, Britain, and the Soviet Union (who'd been fighting Germany since Hitler's invasion the previous June); and the Axis powers led by Germany, Italy, and Japan.

Churchill knew there would be dark days ahead. He recognized the suffering caused by war. Still, the night after Pearl Harbor, he recalled, "I went to bed and slept the sleep of the saved and the thankful."

The Yanks were finally coming.

If You Were a Code and Cipher Breaker: Deciphering a Message

Now that you understand the five clues for breaking into enciphered messages, it's time to put them to use. Let's say the message reads:

UIF FOFNZ BSF PO XBZ DPNF BU PODF BMM

TRU GPS BUUBDL UPOJHIU

The first thing we notice is the message is broken into ordinary words, not five-letter groups. This will make things easier, especially as the message contains two, two-letter words. Two-letter words are sometimes easy to guess. So let's get to work.

First, make a list of letters in the alphabet. Alongside each letter, put the number of times that letter appears in the message.

A	H—1	O—4
B—6	I—2	P—5
C	J—1	Q
D—3	K	R
E	L—1	S—2
F—7	M—2	T—1
G—1	N—2	U—7
	V	
	W	
	X—1	
	Y	
	Z—2	

We find there are no As in the message; there are six Bs; and so on.

We also see that F and U appear most often in the message. Each appears seven times. So probably either F or U stands for that most common letter, E. Now we begin our trial and error guessing method, by which all ciphers are solved.

First, we copy the enciphered message on a sheet of paper, leaving plenty of room between lines. Then we put an E below every F in the enciphered message. If that proves wrong, we will try putting the E below every U in the message instead.

UIF FOFNZ BSF PO XBZ DPNF BU PODF BMM
E E E   E   E   E

TFU GPS BUUBDL UPOJHIU
E

Now we look at the last of the most frequent letters and see that T is the next most common letter after E. So we decide that if F stands for E, maybe the U's stand for T's. So we put a T below every U in the message.

UIF FOFNZ BSF PO XBZ DPNF BU PODF BMM
T E E E   E   E T   E

TFU GPS BUUBDL UPOJHIU
E T   T T   T   T

So far it looks hopeful. In fact, we have two new clues. One is in the first word that reads T__E. It can't be TAE or TBE or

TCE because there are no such words. But if we continue on through the alphabet, trying each letter in turn in the empty space, we come to THE. Those three letters may also turn out to be TIE or TOE. But THE is a far more common word than either of those, so let's try it first.

Our second clue is in the little two-letter word written BU. Since we've decided to decipher the U as a T, it now reads: __T. The word must be either AT or IT, because there are no ordinary two-letter words that end in T except for those two. Let's experiment with AT first, and fill in A's for every B in the message. Now we have:

UIF FOFNZ BSF PO XBZ DPNF BU PODF BMM
THE E E   A E   A   E AT   E A

TFU GPS BUUBDL UPOJHIU
ET   AT TA T   HT

Now, we have another clue in the three-letter word BSF, partly deciphered into A__E. If we try filling in the empty space with various letters, we find that the word ARE is more common than any of the other words we can make, so let's write in R in place of S as an experiment. And let's write R's for every other S in the message. Now we have:

```
UIF FOFNZ BSF PO XBZ DPNF BU PODF BMM
THE E E   ARE   A    E AT    E A

TFU GPS BUUBDL UPOJHIU
ET   R AT TA   T    HT
```

Do you see it? Another clue has appeared in the word BUUBDL. We have deciphered the B's into A's, and the U's into T's, so we have ATTA__ __. A good guess would be that word is ATTACK, so let's put C's for the D's in the message, and K for the L, too:

```
UIF FOFNZ BSF PO XBZ DPNF BU PODF BMM
THE E E   ARE   A C   E AT    CE A

TFU GPS BUUBDL UPOJHIU
ET   R AT TACK T     HT
```

Now go back to the list of most frequent letters. The letters E, T, and A, usually the most frequent, are deciphered. The list tells us the next most frequent letter is likely to be O, and the one after that is N. If we look at the count we made of the most frequent letters in our cipher message, we find that the fourth most frequent one is P and the fifth is O. Let's see what happens if we decipher every P as O and every O as N. Now we have:

UIF FOFNZ BSF PO XBZ DPNF BU PODF BMM
THE ENE   ARE ON A CO E AT ONCE A
TFU GPS BUUBDL UPOJHIU
ET OR AT TACK TON HT

Look! Our little two-letter word PO is ON, and the four-letter word PODF is ONCE. We can feel pretty confident that we were right about the P and O.

Now the sixth, seventh, and eighth words of the message read CO__E AT ONCE. Surely that is COME AT ONCE. And if we deciphered that N into an M, we can do the same for the N in the second word, giving us ENEM. That word must be ENEMY. Now we can put a Y in place of the other Z in the three-letter ciphered XBS, which will give us __AY. Let's take a careful look at the first eight words of the message. They read THE ENEMY ARE ON __AY COME AT ONCE. __AY must be WAY.

Now let's look at the two words before the last word of the enciphered message. They read __OR ATTACK. By trying different letters of the alphabet in the blank space we find that __OR could be FOR or NOR, but FOR ATTACK sounds more likely, so let's make the enciphered G an F.

What about that curious little word BMM? So far we know only that the first letter is A. Let's look at the list of the most frequent double letters and see if we can decide what the MM stands for. The only word that really makes sense is ALL. So let's write it that way. Now we have:

UIF FOFNZ BSF PO XBZ DPNF BU PODF BMM
THE ENEMY ARE ON WAY COME AT ONCE AL L
TFU GPS BUUBDL UPOJHIU
ET FOR ATTACK TON HT

The whole message is deciphered now except for the two words that read __ET and TON__HT. We look at our list of most frequent letters again, and in the list we find that I and S are the two most frequent letters after the ones we've already used—E, T, A, O, N, and R. So let's see if an I or S fits into any of those blanks.

Soon we discover that our whole message reads:

UIF FOFNZ BSF PO XBZ DPNF BU PODF BMM
THE ENEMY ARE ON WAY COME AT ONCE ALL
TFU GPS BUUBDL UPOJHIU
SET FOR ATTACK TONIGHT

We've broken the cipher! Of course, we were lucky in deciphering it because we made the right choice in the beginning. What if we'd put E's in place of all the U's at the start? We would have worked for quite a while before even realizing we were on the wrong track. Deciphering this code would have been much harder.

If the Nazis had sent this message, they would have made it harder still by breaking it into groups of five letters. Our original encrypted message would have looked like this:

UIFFO FNZBS FPOXB ZDPNF BUPOD FBMMT FUGPS BUUBD

LUPOJ HIUXX (Notice the nulls in the last grouping.)

Is it any wonder the Nazis used this tactic?

As a cryptographer you will need to be patient and dogged. You will need the willingness to try again and again. And you will need to work quickly. You have only twenty-four hours to break a Nazi cipher. That's because German commanders change the cipher every day at a few minutes past midnight. If you do manage to break today's cipher, congratulations! Just know that tomorrow a new cipher will need to be broken . . . and the day after that . . . and the day after that . . . until the war ends.

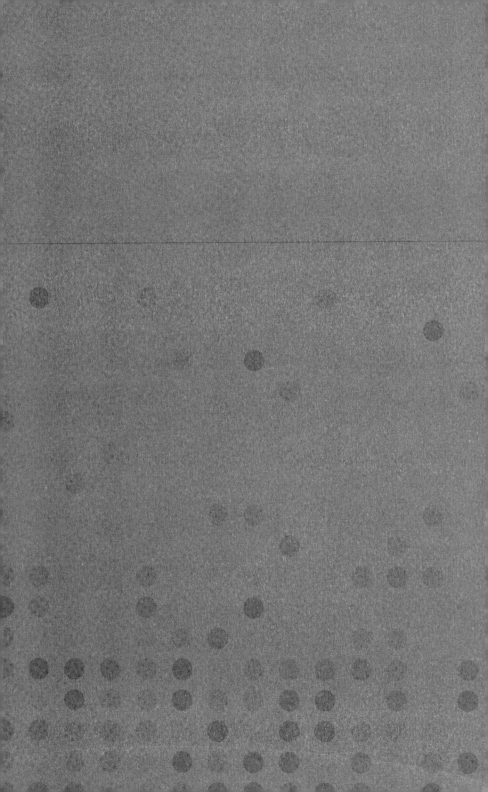

BOMBES AND CODEBOOKS

16

LEAP OF FAITH

Can you keep a secret?"

Seventeen-year-old Diana Payne stared at the Wren officer who interviewed her. What an odd question. Shouldn't the officer be asking about Diana's sailing experience, or something more . . . um . . . naval?

Diana shrugged. "I really don't know."

Her answer didn't put off the officer. She sized up the teenager, noting her height—5′8″.

Just right for Special Duties X.

She told Diana to report to the Wren training camp in New College, Hampstead.

Diana was thrilled. The British government now required by law all able-bodied women to do war work, but there were choices. Females between the ages of seventeen and a half and forty could sign up for military service with the WAAFs (Women's Auxiliary Air Force), the WAACs (Women's Army Auxiliary Corps), the WRNS (Women's Royal Naval Service) or the ATS (Auxiliary Territorial Service), Civilian women (like Sarah, Jane, and Mavis) were considered part of the FO (Foreign Office), while other nonmilitary women did essential jobs like farming, nursing, teaching, or factory work. When it had come time for Diana to choose, she'd hotfooted it down to the Wren recruiting office. For as long as she could remember, she'd dreamed of a life at sea. She even had the romantic notion of marrying a sailor.

But life at Wren training camp was not what she'd expected. For two weeks, she marched up and down the parade ground and learned naval etiquette. Then she was "kitted out" with uniform and toiletries and driven—along with twenty-two other brand-new Wrens—to London's Euston train station. She didn't know where she was headed. None of them did.

Diana grabbed a porter's elbow. Could he tell her where this train was going?

The porter grinned. "The Wrens get off at Bletchley."

At the station, a bus met them. They were driven to a moldering country manor sixty miles from the Park called

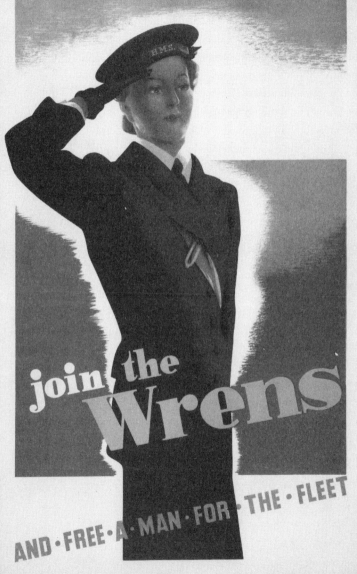

A recruiting poster for the Wrens shows off to good effect the service's crisp and attractive uniform.

Crawley Grange. This would be their billet, one of several large estates that had been requisitioned by the military to house the ever-growing number of Park workers.

It wasn't until the next morning that the new recruits got their first introduction to Bletchley Park. Led into one of the huts, they were met by a stern-faced naval officer. He got right to the point. Their jobs here would be "shift work," he told them, "with very little hope of promotion." It would also require their "complete secrecy." Could they endure that? He looked around. This was their only chance to back out.

Back out of *what*? The new recruits still knew nothing about the job. It seemed "nuts," Diana later admitted, to agree to the unknown. Still, she never considered backing out. Britain needed her. So she faced the mysterious challenge and signed the Official Secrets Act. It was, she admitted, "a leap of faith."

17

BY LEAPS AND BOUNDS AND BASKET RIDES

Bletchley Park kept growing. Churchill had kept his promise, and more and more recruits arrived daily, two-thirds of them female, and most of them teenagers. To accommodate all the people, more buildings were erected. By 1942, there were huts for the telephone exchange (hundreds of calls went in and out of the Park daily), for the mechanics and engineers workshops, for the vehicles and their drivers, for storage of food, for office supplies, and more. It wasn't an orderly development. The Park outgrew itself rapidly, and as more buildings sprang up, the function of existing huts changed again and again. Hut 1, for example, began as a site for wireless radios as well as a sick bay. Later still, it housed firefighting equipment and lavatories. Inside the huts, partitions were put up or pulled down as needed—sometimes while staff still worked in them. "The rooms were always changing shape," recalled one worker. "Once I was typing and suddenly this saw came through the partition and narrowly missed my head!" And still the contractors whacked out structures. "It wasn't a rush," recalled one builder, "it was a panic."

Sarah Norton's Naval Section—both Hut 8 and Hut 4—was moved to a two-story concrete building called Block A. This new structure had a long corridor that ended in a pair of double, swinging doors. Sarah wondered what lay behind them.

One afternoon, at the end of her shift, she had a fun idea. Why not give her friend Jean a ride in the wheeled laundry basket. The basket was normally used to move files. But now, Sarah emptied it of its documents, and Jean climbed in.

Sarah gave it a big push.

The basket shot down the corridor, picking up speed by the second.

Like a hound after a rabbit, Sarah chased it. But before she could catch up, the basket with Jean still in it shot through the double doors.

Panting, Sarah came to a stop. Should she follow?

Moments passed. Then a red-faced Jean shot back out, still in the basket. She'd learned what lay behind the swinging doors—the men's bathroom! A boffin who'd been washing his hands had stopped the basket. Wordlessly, he'd turned it around and pushed it—and Jean—back out.

It didn't take Commander Crawford long to hear about the incident. He ordered the teens into his office, where he scolded them severely. He vowed never to let them work together again.

Jean plastered a false look of repentance onto her face.

Sarah blinked back fake tears.

Commander Crawford caved.

Soon, the two went back to sharing shifts.

Sarah was glad for the return of her friend's company. Still, she felt itchy and confined. "I seemed to be growing out of the Index Room like a child whose socks have shrunk," she admitted. But what could she do about it? Higher-ups had stuck her here. There seemed no way to escape the endless cross-referencing.

18

CIPHERS AND ROMANCE

That spring, mathematician Keith Batey was transferred to the Cottage. Mavis couldn't believe her luck. She'd been trying to catch his attention for months now!

It had all begun the previous fall. One night she'd had some problems with an intercept. "So I went over to Hut 6 and found one of the mathematicians there and he very kindly volunteered to help me," Mavis explained later.

That kind volunteer had been Keith. Returning to the Cottage, the two had sipped coffee while trying to solve the problem.

Mavis's attention, however, kept drifting. She found herself thinking Keith was "rather nice." She decided to test him by purposely dropping her pencil. She hoped he'd gallantly bend down and pick it up for her.

He didn't. Instead, he'd stared down at the object, and then back at Mavis. "You've dropped your pencil," he said.

With a sigh, Mavis picked it up and went back to work. "It was *not*," she later admitted, "love at first sight."

But now she was working with him every day. And she'd caught him staring at her when he thought she wasn't looking. Did Keith think she was "rather nice," too? She forced her attention back to the intercept in front of her. The Spy Enigma beckoned. Romance would have to wait.

19

THE BOMBES

Diana Payne's dreams of a life at sea shattered the moment she stepped into Hut 11A. A long, windowless room, the place managed to be both cavernous and claustrophobic. Nine "mechanical monsters," as Diana called them, stood in its center.

"They were bronze-colored cabinets, each about eight feet tall and seven feet wide," Diana recalled. "The front held rows of colored wheels, five inches in diameter and three inches deep. . . . The letters of the alphabet had been painted around each one." The back of the machine "almost defied description—a mass of dangling plugs on rows of letters and numbers."

The Hut's supervisor provided a name for the machines:

Bombes. Designed by Alan Turing, and partly based on an earlier machine developed by the Polish cryptologists, the Bombe's purpose was to speed up the process of breaking the day's Enigma settings. And speed was of the essence. With 159 quintillion possible combinations each day, breaking the settings by hand was far too time-consuming. The Bombe, however, could race through millions of possibilities and discover the settings—sometimes in as little as fifteen to eighteen minutes (but sometimes much longer, even hours). With the day's settings revealed, the intercepts could be quickly decrypted and the intelligence passed on . . . often with enough time to be acted upon.

Every day, more Bombes were being built. And every single one needed a two-girl team to operate it. That's where the Wrens came in, supplying the Park with well-trained, intelligent, and *tall* girls. "I realized then," Diana said, "that I was never going to get a glimpse of the sea or sailors."

That day was the beginning of over three years of working on watches of four weeks' duration: eight a.m. to four p.m. the first week; four p.m. to midnight the second; and midnight to eight a.m. the third. The fourth week was three days of alternate shifts, eight hours on and eight hours off, ending in a much-needed four days' leave.

AMPLIFIER CHASSIS   RELAY CHASSIS   NEON L

REGULATOR
CHASSIS

THYRATRON
CHASSIS

BANK
SWITCHES

WHEEL
BANK
CONNECTORS

A LEVEL
WHEEL
BANKS

B LEVEL

C LEVEL

D LEVEL

A.C.
MAIN
SWITCH

SOLA
REGULATOR

REWIND
MOTOR

CHAIN
COUPLING

ZERO

MAGNETIC
REWIND
CLUTCH

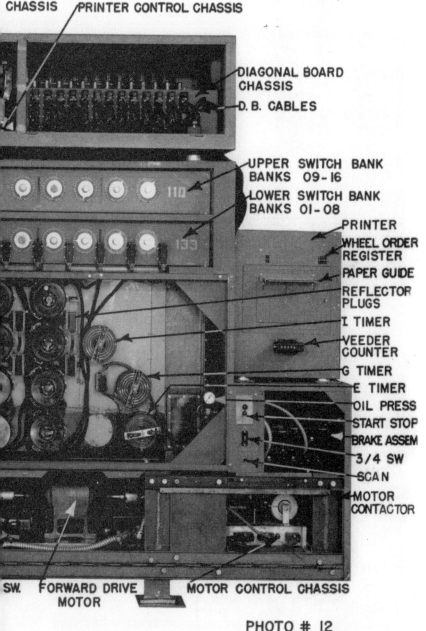

CHASSIS PRINTER CONTROL CHASSIS

DIAGONAL BOARD CHASSIS

D. B. CABLES

UPPER SWITCH BANK BANKS 09-16

LOWER SWITCH BANK BANKS 01-08

PRINTER

WHEEL ORDER REGISTER

PAPER GUIDE

REFLECTOR PLUGS

I TIMER

VEEDER COUNTER

G TIMER

E TIMER

OIL PRESS

START STOP

BRAKE ASSEM

3/4 SW

SCAN

MOTOR CONTACTOR

SW. FORWARD DRIVE MOTOR

MOTOR CONTROL CHASSIS

PHOTO # 12
N-530 BOMBE
FRONT

A front view of the Bombe with all its parts labeled.

N-530 BOMBE
SECOND DECK   BUILDING 4
MAY 25, 1945

A female staff member makes adjustments to a Bombe.

At the start of each shift, a supervisor assigned Diana and another Wren to a Bombe, and gave them a "menu." The menu was a complicated diagram of letters and links with various drawn lines that looked like a puzzle. The menu explained how the Bombe should be plugged up, with the cords in the machine's back corresponding to the positions on the menus. Additionally, the menu specified the order of the colored wheels. All this had to be done quickly and accurately. If Diana didn't follow the menu exactly, if she made even the tiniest error, the Bombe would never find the correct settings.

It was exhausting work. Hoisting the heavy wheels caused Diana's arms to ache, and her fingers were pinched purple by the heavy clips that snapped each drum in place. Plugging up the back required wrestling with a nest of copper wires without letting them touch. Occasionally, sparks flew. And a couple of times a day, the machine gave her an electrical shock. Operating it, Diana decided, was like caring for a cranky mechanical monster.

Finally, she started it up, and the Bombe began running through all the possible settings. Mishaps frequently occurred. Sometimes, the wheels needed realignment. Sometimes, Diana had to reach inside with tweezers to separate

This modern-day replica shows what the back of the Bombe looked like, with its complex cables and plugs.

wires that had moved too close together. And always, the Bombe's spindles needed oiling. The gooey stuff seeped onto Diana's fingers and dripped onto her shoes. The acrid smell of warm oil filled her nostrils and permeated her hair and clothing. She could smell it on herself even after a bath. She could smell it on the other Wrens, too. Her hands became calloused, and her fingers were covered with tiny cuts.

And then there was the noise. The Bombes sounded like the clattering of a thousand knitting needles. This made talking with the other Wrens impossible. Diana spent her eight-hour shifts feeling isolated despite there being eighteen other girls in the room.

Then suddenly, the Bombe would come to a stop. This indicated that the machine had found the settings . . . well . . . most of the time. Occasionally, the Bombe produced "false stops," meaning it hadn't found the right setting. To verify the Bombe's answer, Diana's partner would check it on a piece of equipment similar to a Typex, called the "checking machine." First, she would set up the checking machine with the positions found by the Bombe. Then she would start typing. If the text came out in German, that meant the Bombe's answer was right.

An up-close view of the checking machine.

In that case, the supervisor shouted, "Job's up! Strip machines!"

And Diana's Bombe—as well as any others that had been working on that particular day's setting—was stopped and unplugged. But the work wasn't over. Even as the supervisor telephoned the Bombe's answer to higher-ups, a brand-new menu was arriving in Hut 11A.

After just six weeks of working on the Bombes, Diana Payne looked haggard. Worse, she felt lonely and depressed. In those rare moments when her mind wasn't occupied by the mechanical monsters, she thought about the men she knew who were fighting in Europe, North Africa, and the Pacific. Was her work vital to their safety? It had to be. Otherwise, how could she keep going? Without the belief that she was doing something important to defeat the Nazis, admitted Diana, the job would have "driven [her] nuts."

She also daydreamed about her next day off, when she'd take the train to London, or see a movie or visit friends. Most of all, she daydreamed about sleep. Caring for the Bombe took a real physical and emotional toll. And Diana wasn't the only Wren affected.

One of the girls in her billet—an eighteen-year-old named Sally—had been put to bed in the sick bay. She'd spent days there, sleeping. She rarely woke up, and ate almost nothing. Eventually, her supervisor gave her a special two-week pass. Sally went home. She returned refreshed, and went right back to the Bombes.

Many others experienced sleeplessness, hand tremors, loss of appetite, and nervousness. Some had breakdowns. Most worked on the edge of mental exhaustion. The long hours, the noise of the rotating wheels, and the intensity of the work put an enormous strain on the Wrens.

"Working on the monster machines was soul-destroying work," admitted Diana.

(20)

LISTENING AND TAPPING

At the Withernsea Y Station, Patricia Owtram still spent four-hour shifts listing to static and snatching German messages from the air. "I didn't find it too difficult to concentrate no matter what the hour," she later claimed. Still, those four-to-eight a.m. shifts were grinding. Rolling out of her bunk, she pulled on a sweater and bell bottoms before shuffling down the hallway to the watchroom. A Wren from the previous shift would press a mug of hot chocolate into Patricia's hand, and fill her in on any noteworthy events. Then the still-sleepy Patricia put on her headphones and began her search of the Kriegsmarine's known radio frequencies.

Allied ships in the Atlantic were having a terrible time

with the German Navy. U-boats prowled the sea in what Nazis called "wolf packs," sinking Allied ships with ease. Meanwhile, German destroyers laid sea mines, making Allied crossings even more dangerous. Any message Patricia intercepted could be vitally important.

But interception wasn't always easy. The German ships stayed quiet as long as possible. They wanted to stay hidden as badly as Patricia and the other Y station listeners wanted to hear them. When the ships finally did use their radios, they changed the frequency in hopes of frustrating anyone listening in. Not knowing which frequency the Nazis were transmitting on meant Patricia had to search for it. Back and forth, slowly, with ears straining, she turned the dials.

Despite constant searching, there were times when she heard nothing for an entire shift. Worse, sometimes she heard nothing for days on end. Was she doing something wrong? It was always a relief when the rapid staccato of Morse code once again filled her earphones.

Her days, however, weren't entirely about eavesdropping. In her spare time Patricia took long walks along the seashore, went to the cinema, and . . . tap-danced!

She'd taken it up after a villager arrived at the station with a box full of tap shoes. Patricia and the other girls had immediately seized on this strange gift. Laughing, they tapped their way up and down the narrow staircase. They formed chorus lines in their dorm rooms, pushing the beds out of the way of their high-kicking legs. They even practiced routines in the attic, although they never performed for anyone but themselves. How wonderful it felt to act a little silly. How nice to feel like a carefree teenager again.

Some nights, as Patricia tapped away in the attic, she heard Nazi bombers flying over the station. Then all silliness fell away, and she murmured a prayer for the people who were in the Germans' sights.

Would the war ever end?

(21)

THE WHOLE PICTURE

Each of the teenagers—Jane, Mavis, Sarah, and Diana—wrestled with just a single, small piece of the Bletchley Park puzzle. They didn't know what anyone else was working on. They couldn't see the *whole* picture. What was the route of an enemy message? Only Park officials knew all eight steps. They were:

One: The enemy transmits a message using wireless signals (radio). The message is encrypted, sometimes using machines like Enigma. The encrypted message is then sent via Morse code.

Two: People like Patricia Owtram who are working in Britain's network of secret listening bases (Y stations) intercept the message. They copy it down.

Three: The message is sent to Bletchley Park.

Four: Cryptographers at Bletchley Park like Mavis Lever and the boffins systematically break the encrypted message's cipher settings. This is done in different ways, sometimes with the help of state-of-the-art machines like the Bombes (run by Wrens like Diana Payne). All cipher breaking, however, requires human brainpower.

Five: Once cryptographers break into the cipher settings, all the encrypted messages for that day's setting can be deciphered. For Enigma ciphers, Typex machines operated by young women like Jane Hughes are used. The deciphered messages come out on a long, thin strip of paper that is cut and glued onto the back of the original.

Six: The deciphered messages are in many different languages—German, Japanese, Italian, and more. They are handed over to teams of translators who put them all into English.

Seven: The translated messages are sent to the Index Room, where young women like Sarah Norton scan them for key words, names, and locations. This information, after being written on index cards, is cross-referenced to create an in-depth picture of the enemy's movements.

Eight: The messages, deciphered and translated, are now top secret intelligence. Higher-ups at Bletchley Park send this intelligence to the relevant people—politicians and military brass. What becomes of the intelligence is out of Bletchley Park's hands. British leaders and commanders will decide if and how they will act on the information they've been given.

22

THE BIGGEST ASYLUM IN BRITAIN

Gwen Davies saw the war as a chance to get away from her parents and have a life of her own. So on her eighteenth birthday in May 1942, she quit school and joined the Women's Auxiliary Air Force (WAAF). She envisioned herself working on plane engines, or maybe even learning to fly.

WAAF officers had other ideas. They summoned the teen to an interview at the Air Ministry in London.

Gwen, who lived a hundred miles away in the seaside village of Bournemouth, found the prospect of the trip thrilling. She made big plans.

First she would go to a shop on Regent Street that sold underwear made from captured German parachute silk.

(The underclothes supplied by the WAAFs were itchy and bulky.)

Next she would walk around the National Gallery looking at the paintings and acting art savvy and grown-up.

Then she would take herself to a late lunch at the British Restaurant, where for just a few pennies she could get a hearty helping of beans on toast.

Only then would she stroll over to the Air Ministry for her interview, which had been scheduled for four thirty p.m.

Gwen did it all. By the time she squeezed through the Ministry's sandbagged entrance, she felt sick. The beans weren't sitting well, and she was exhausted.

Now a commander appeared and handed her a printed sheet. He asked her to translate it.

Gwen recognized the language. She'd taken German in school. But the article was about new research in aviation, and it was full of technical terms she didn't know. Besides, she felt queasy. She stumbled through a few paragraphs.

Annoyed, the commander snatched back the paper. She was wasting his time. Why had WAAF officers recommended her? Her German stank.

"I bet my [German] vocabulary's better than yours," a miserable Gwen replied. She started to sing him a song in the language when suddenly she groaned. "I think I'm going to be sick."

Without blinking, the commander pushed his wastebasket toward her.

The teenager vomited into it. She felt sure she'd failed her interview.

But the commander seemed unfazed by her behavior. He posted her to the wireless station at Chicksands.

Gwen whooped right there in his office. She was going to be a radio operator!

But days later when she arrived at the station, the commanding officer there said, "Don't put your kit down." He was sending her someplace else.

"Where?" asked Gwen.

The officer didn't answer. Instead, he turned to a driver. "Are you going to blindfold her," he asked, "or take her in a covered van?"

"Well, the van's ready," replied the driver. He picked up Gwen's kit.

She nervously followed.

In the back of the vehicle, Gwen's fears grew. The windows of the van had been blacked out, and she was separated from the driver by a wooden board. All alone, her imagination ran wild. Was she being kidnapped? Had she been mistaken for a German spy?

Finally the van stopped, and the driver opened the door. She found herself standing alone outside a guardhouse, her kit at her feet, as the van drove away. Gwen approached one of the sentries.

"Can't come in here," said the first guard. "Got no pass."

"Look," said Gwen, whose fear had turned to anger. "I don't know where I am, and I don't know what I'm supposed to do."

A second guard came up to her. He told her to go to the hut at the left of the gates. "Somebody will come and see you." Then he added, "And if you want to know where you are, you're at Bletchley Park."

"And if you want to know what that is," added the first guard with a snort of laughter, "it's the biggest lunatic asylum in Britain."

23

CIPHERS AND WORD GAMES

Enigma? In all her time at Bletchley Park, Gwen Davies would never once hear the word. She was assigned to Hut 10, Block A, where she worked at unraveling all the Luftwaffe's "low-grade ciphers." These were communications *not* encrypted by Enigma. Rather, they were messages encrypted by using a cipher book. A cipher book showed the secret cipher for every letter of plain text. If both the sender and the receiver had a copy of this book, they could easily communicate. Information sent using cipher books wasn't considered high-grade intelligence by the Park's top brass. But it was still valuable. From these messages, Bletchley Park might learn the location of air bases,

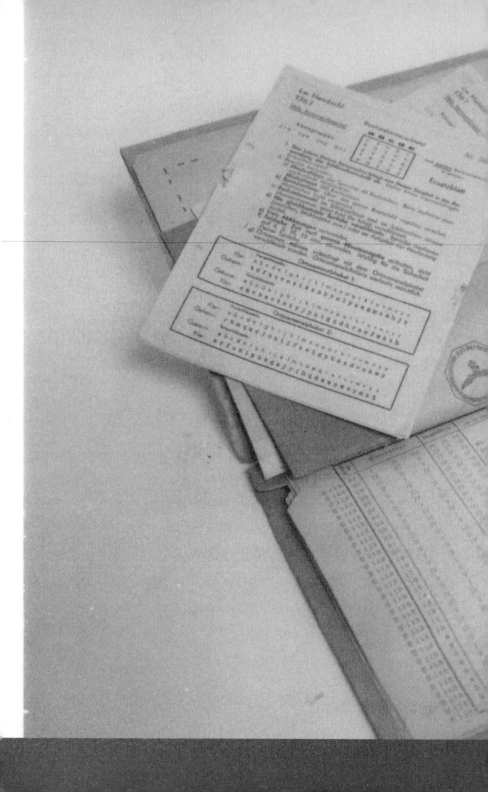

A captured Luftwaffe cipher book.

the types of aircraft in a formation, or the number of flying units.

Gwen dove headfirst into her work. Using a cipher book taken from a downed German aircraft, she converted encrypted text into raw clumps of German that she handed to the translator.

She didn't work alone. Rather, a team of four others worked with her. Bending over an encrypted message, she might suddenly see a German letter coming out.

"I've got an E," she would holler.

"I've got a B," someone else on the team would call out.

Then everyone would put their solutions on the chalkboard.

BE _ _ _ _ _

Using their language skills, as well as intuition, the team brainstormed to fill in the gaps.

"BERICHT," someone would eventually shout.

It meant "report" in German.

With the first word in the message solved, they'd move to the second word, then the third, and the fourth, until the entire message was deciphered.

It was, admitted Gwen, "all rather fun, like an endless game of hangman."

24

SURPRISING NEWS

In June, Mavis visited Dilly Knox. Too sick to leave his house, he was nonetheless working on a top secret project that even Mavis knew nothing about. But she had a secret, too. For the past months she'd quietly been dating Keith Batey. And now . . . they were engaged! She showed Dilly her ring.

Was the twenty-year-old taking a step she'd regret? Dilly wanted to be sure. "You do realize mathematicians can be unimaginative," he said.

"Well, this one's not like that," she replied.

Dilly let the matter drop, and congratulated her. When was the wedding?

Mavis wasn't sure. Like many young men at Bletchley Park, Keith wanted to actively be in war. He had friends on the front line and felt guilty about his safe job in the countryside. To the higher-ups at the Park, he insisted that women were perfectly capable of breaking ciphers. Just look at Mavis! They didn't need men to get the work done. And he wanted to do his bit by going off to war.

His bosses had blanched. Put one of their top Enigma cipher breakers at risk of being captured and possibly giving away Bletchley's secrets? Never.

But Keith had worn them down, and eventually a compromise was reached. The mathematician could go to war *if* he agreed to join the Royal Navy's air service, rather than the Royal Air Force. That way, reasoned the top brass, if he got shot down, it would be over water. Instead of being captured, he'd most likely drown.

Keith had been overjoyed.

Mavis wasn't.

Now she told Dilly she hoped they could tie the knot before Keith shipped off to Canada for his pilot's training. But who knew? War was so unpredictable.

(25)

LOOSE LIPS

Jane Hughes sat in the canteen, pushing a stewed prune around her plate, feeling gloomy. The stress. The unending work. The secrecy. "It could sometimes be oppressive," she admitted.

Suddenly, a quarrel erupted at a nearby table. Jane couldn't believe her ears. Two of her colleagues from Hut 6, Mary and Gillian, were arguing about who knew the most secrets.

"And I bet you didn't know that it was Hut 8 that broke the codes in North Africa . . ." exclaimed Mary at the top of her voice.

"Well, that's very interesting, but I bet you didn't know that we probably knew about the bombing of Pearl Harbor before it happened," Gillian countered loudly.

Everyone in the lunchroom froze. Even Mary and Gillian seemed to realize they'd gone too far. They looked around to see who'd heard them, then hurried back to the Hut. Jane followed.

She had just settled back at her Typex machines when a furious supervisor appeared. Beside her walked two military policemen. She pointed at Mary and Gillian. "I cannot believe . . . the gossip you indulged in at lunch," she declared. "You have signed the Official Secrets Act and agreed to abide by it . . . You have broken that trust and I have no other course of action than to dismiss you from your posts immediately. Gather your personal effects and leave."

Both young women begged for another chance. "We didn't mean anything by it," cried Mary.

But the supervisor remained unmoved. She reminded them that the punishment could have been much worse. They *could* have been sent to prison. With that, the military police escorted them off the property.

But the supervisor wasn't through yet. She whirled on Jane and the others. "Ladies, let this incident serve as a warning to you all that we will not tolerate slack behavior or loose talk."

The incident added to Jane's already cloudy mood. And

SECRECY

1/3/19

1 May 1/42

This may seem a simple matter. It should be. But repeated experience has proved that it is not. Even for the cleverest of us; even for the least important. Month after month instances have occurred where workers at B.P. have been heard casually saying outside B.P. things that are dangerous.

It is not enough to know that you must not hint at these things outside. It must be uppermost in your mind every hour that you talk to outsiders. Even the most trivial-seeming things matter. The enemy does not get his intelligence by great scoops, but from a whisper here, a tiny detail there. Therefore:—

DO NOT TALK AT MEALS. There are the waitresses and others who may not be in the know regarding your own particular work.

DO NOT TALK IN THE TRANSPORT. There are the drivers who should not be in the know.

DO NOT TALK TRAVELLING. Indiscretions have been overheard on Bletchley platform. They do not grow less serious further off.

DO NOT TALK IN YOUR BILLET. Why expect your hosts who are not pledged to secrecy to be more discreet than you, who are?

DO NOT TALK BY YOUR OWN FIRESIDE, whether here or on leave. If you are indiscreet and tell your own folks, they may see no reason why they should not do likewise. They are not in a position to know the consequences and have received no guidance. Moreover, if one day invasion came, as it perfectly well may, Nazi brutality might stop at nothing to wring from those that you care for, secrets that you would give anything, then, to have saved them from knowing. Their only safety will lie in utter ignorance of your work.

BE CAREFUL EVEN IN YOUR HUT. Cleaners and maintenance staff have ears, and are human.

There is nothing to be gained by chatter but the satisfaction of idle vanity, or idle curiosity: there is everything to be lost—the very existence of our work, the lives of others, even the War itself.

People will always be curious. They can always learn something from your answers, *if* you answer, even though you only answer 'Yes' or 'No'. Do not suggest, as is so easy, and so flattering to human vanity, that you are doing something very important and very 'hush-hush'. Far too many people in England know that about Bletchley Park already. If ever the Germans come to know it, we may find ourselves a German 'Target for To-night'. There are drawbacks to publicity.

The only way, then, is to cut the conversation short. For example:—

Question. What are you doing now?
Answer. Working for the Foreign Office (or other Ministry as appropriate).
Question. But what do you *do*?
Answer. Oh—work.

A gay reticence in that vein will win you far more real respect from anyone worth respecting, than idle indiscretion or self-important airs of mystery.

There is an English proverb none the worse for being seven centuries old:—

Wicked tongue breaketh bone,
Though the tongue itself hath none.

I hereby promise that no word of mine shall betray, however slightly, the great trust placed in me.

Signed

O.U.P. Form No. 14.

Notices like this one were posted all around the Park as a reminder to staff of the oath they swore to secrecy.

as the weeks passed, her workload, already heavy, reached torrent level. Intercepts surged in. Some days, Jane felt like she was drowning in them. This, of course, was due to the success of Y stations in intercepting German messages, as well as the increasing ability of Bletchley Park to decipher them. Astonishingly, that summer Hut 6 broke into twenty-six different Luftwaffe and Wehrmacht Enigma settings *each and every day*. That came to about twenty-five thousand decrypts per month. No wonder Jane's fingernails were nothing more than nubs.

Did Jane wish she could share her feelings with others at the Park? She could have used the support. But the Official Secrets Act made sharing impossible. When it came to her emotional well-being, Jane was completely on her own.

26

NO ESCAPING THE MONSTERS

After just six months, Diana Payne was leaving Bletchley Park. Unfortunately, she wouldn't be leaving the Bombes. The "mechanical monsters" had proven their worth. More were needed, along with more Wrens to run them. Bletchley Park did not have that sort of space, and so dozens of Bombes were installed in five nearby country estates. Commandeered by the military, these estates housed not only the machines but the Wrens as well.

One of these estates—Wavendon Manor—became Diana's new home. The sixteenth-century, two-story mansion was lovely. But Diana and the other Wrens did not get to live inside. They billeted in the old stable block, a long room furnished with bunk beds. Cold in the winter and hot in the summer, the stable also housed nesting swallows in its rafters and mice in its walls. It had no indoor toilet facilities. Instead, the Wrens had to use a primitive outhouse.

A short walk across muddy grounds took Diana to two dark, windowless huts set away from the main house. Here fourteen Bombes ran around the clock. There were twenty-two Wrens on watch. Two were duty Wrens whose job it was to brew tea twice during the shift, and—if it was a night watch—to make supper, usually bread and cheese.

(Their other meals came from Bletchley Park in a large container since they didn't have cooking facilities.)

The house and garden at Wavendon Manor. While lovely, it was off-limits for the Wrens.

A petty officer supervised. She stayed constantly in touch with Bletchley Park by telephone. Additionally, a leading Wren sat in each hut and issued the menus, or "wheel orders," as they were sometimes called. Diana called them "woes."

The nickname seemed apt.

27

THE HAPPY COUPLE
AND A GRIM REMINDER

Even the gray November weather couldn't dim Mavis's happiness. In a London registry office, she and Keith took their marriage vows. Afterward, they hurried away to a brief honeymoon in the Lake District. How annoying it was for Mavis when Keith's brother, Herbert, came to visit them. Keith spent one of their three precious days playing chess with his brother. But Mavis quickly forgave him. There wasn't time for petty grievances.

After the honeymoon, Keith sailed to Canada. Mavis worried about the ship crossing. The Atlantic Ocean was infested with Nazi U-boats, and since US entry into the war, they constantly patrolled America's east coast. She hoped the German Naval Section was breaking into those U-boat encrypts. Would anyone in that section give her information about his ship's progress? Mavis knew better than to ask. The only thing to do was get back to work.

Gwen Davies's job stopped being a fun word game the day after Christmas. That's when her supervisor laid a folder on her desk. It contained a Nazi cipher book. Captured just hours earlier from a downed German airplane, it had been rushed to Bletchley Park. Now, Gwen picked it up . . . then dropped it back on her desk in horror. The book's cover had a huge bloodstain on it. She discovered the inside pages did, too, once she got up the courage to open it. When she drew away her hand, it was sticky with blood.

The teenager felt sick. "I realized then that somewhere this German airman was still bleeding, maybe dying, while I was [translating] his cipher book," she said. "*That* really did bring the war very close."

If You Were a Code and Cipher Breaker: Cribs

Imagine you are setting up a password that requires just four numbers and no letters. This means there would be ten thousand different possible combinations available to set up that password.

Now imagine you reveal two of those numbers to someone. Guess what? You've just reduced the possible combinations to one hundred. It wouldn't take a person long to break into your password.

Now imagine you've added lots of uppercase and lowercase letters to your password, as well as symbols and numbers. Say your password is now ten characters long. It would take a fast computer a good while to break your password, because there are so many possible combinations. Could someone ever crack your password with a computer? Could they do it by hand? It's possible, especially if you've included the name of your dog in that password, or your birthday. The password breaker might guess that, and with enough trial and error, she might get some of your password correct.

At Bletchley Park, this guess is called a **crib**. And in the case of both German and Italian Enigma messages, these "cribs" come in the form of predictable words or phrases that are used in the transmissions. "Nothing to report" is a common way for a German Enigma operator to start a message. "Heil Hitler" is often found at message's end. Routine phrases used in weather reports can also become cribs. "Weather for the night" is often found in Enigma enciphered messages. So is "beacon lit as ordered," and "situation eastern channel." By guessing that these cribs are included in a message, you might eventually find your way into the Enigma settings. But guessing isn't enough. You have to verify that your crib is valid. Let's discover how:

Imagine that you've guessed the crib SECRET MESSAGE is included in this enciphered text.

H Q E Y S A W Q S T N T L G K P E S R C V L

It could be that the enciphered text starts with SECRET MESSAGE. In that case the crib would be:

HQEYSAWQSTNTLGKPESRCVL
SECRETMESSAGE

But how do you know that's valid? Maybe the crib is in the enciphered text at a different position, like this:

HQEYSAWQSTNTLGKPESRCVL
SECRETMESSAGE

Your job, once you suspect an enciphered text contains a crib, is to identify the crib's starting point. How do you do this? By using what you know about the ways in which the Enigma machine works. Remember that the Enigma machine will *never* encipher a letter as itself. If the operator presses the letter S on the machine's keyboard, the letter Q or F might pop up on the lamp board, but not the letter S; the letter F might become a Z or an A, but never F, and so forth. Using this knowledge allows us to discard most crib positions:

1.   H Q E Y S A W Q **S** T N T L G K P E S R C V L
    S E C R E T M E **S** S A G E

2.   H Q **E** Y S A W Q S T N T L G K P E S R C V L
    S **E** C R E T M E S S A G E

3.   H Q E Y S A W Q S T N T L **G** K P E S R C V L
    S E C R E T M E S S A **G** E

4.   H Q E Y S A W Q S T N T L G K P E S R C V L
    S E C R E T M E S S A G E

5.   H Q E Y **S** A W Q S T N T L G K P **E** S R C V L
    S E C R E T M E S S A G **E**

You can see that most crib positions can be discarded, leaving only one possible crib (number four). The crib and its position will be used to create menus for the Bombe machines that will result in discovering the day's Enigma settings. Remember, there will always be unsuccessfully deciphered messages. This typically happens when the assumed crib—despite all signs to the contrary—is wrong, or its position is off.

1943

SLOGGING, GRINDING
WAR WORK

28

LEISURE AND LIES

What was a girl to do for fun once her shift ended?

Recalled one Park worker, "There were concerts and recitals; chamber music classes and operatic evenings; poetry readings . . . clubs for Scottish country dancing and jazz; language courses, films and lectures and plays, revues and dances. There really was something for most people."

Jane Hughes turned to music. Once a week she gathered with other singers around the grand piano in the mansion's ballroom. Herbert Murrell directed this choral society. It didn't bother Jane that she didn't know—and would never know—what Murrell did at Bletchley Park. What mattered

Park staff take a break from their work to play cricket on the grass in front of the manor house.

to her was what he'd done *before* the war. In those days, he'd been head of music at the British Broadcasting Corporation. Now he passed on his expertise to the group. On summer evenings, they performed by the lake, and during the winter they gave recitals in the ballroom. Jane—who had an excellent singing voice—often soloed during these performances. Music became a bright spot in her hectic, overworked life.

Mavis bicycled far into the countryside as an antidote to work. Gwen played a lot of tennis on the Bletchley Park tennis courts. Both frequented the small library set up in the house. Gwen sometimes listened to gramophone records in the lounge (also set up in the house). There was chess, darts, and table tennis if either was interested.

Sarah Norton steered clear of it all. At the end of a daytime shift, she often rushed to catch the train to London, an evening dress stuffed into her oversized handbag. Despite the rubble and mess, the city's theaters, restaurants, and dance floors still beckoned.

One night she joined a group of friends at the Claridge Hotel, where the conversation turned to their wartime jobs.

"I am the personal assistant to the admiral in charge of the docks at Portsmouth," bragged one friend.

"I drive a four-star American general in a real Cadillac," boasted a second.

"Well," added a third, "I am the aide to someone very high up in the War office." She looked around at the others to see if they were duly impressed.

They all turned to Sarah. What did she do?'

"It's a secret," said Sarah. "Promise not to tell?"

Her friends leaned in, nodding their agreement.

And Sarah launched into a long-winded, detailed account of how she kept files on those who'd received medals for valor in battle. She babbled on and on, until her friends' faces glazed over with boredom. Soon, they begged her to stop talking.

It was exactly the response Sarah had wanted. Word soon got around that she was deathly dull when discussing her war work, and it was best not to discuss it. Her secrecy problem was solved.

The next morning—before the sun had even risen—Sarah caught the first train back to Bletchley Station, arriving just in time for the start of her next shift. True, she did feel "a bit bleary-eyed." She was also, she admitted, "a touch overdressed."

29

ENDINGS AND BEGINNINGS

In February, Mavis visited Dilly Knox in the hospital. She found him laughing with his brother over a book of collected famous last words called *The Art of Dying*.

Mavis never revealed what the two of them talked about that day. But when she left, Dilly gave her the book. She promised to cherish it.

It was the last time she saw him. He died on February 27 at the age of fifty-eight. "He was skeptical of most things," a friend noted at his funeral, "except those that really matter, that is, affection and reason."

Enough with sticking cards in boxes! Sarah Norton needed to stretch her mind. So on a chilly April morning, she cornered Commander Crawford. Any girl could handle the Index, she told him. But how many of them spoke fluent German? Bletchley Park was wasting her talents.

Crawford saw her point. A week later, he transferred her.

Sarah still remained in Hut 4—German Naval Section— but now she found herself squeezed into a room with a gaggle of much older men who'd studied German in college, and a cluster of older women who gone to finishing schools in Munich and Vienna. They sat around a tall table translating recently deciphered German messages into English.

Female staff translate the decrypts under the watchful eye of a male supervisor.

One of the men pushed a stack of these "fresh decrypts" toward her.

Sarah picked up a pencil and flipped open a German dictionary. The decrypt said something about a U-boat wolf pack. But the entire message wasn't there. Whole chunks of paragraphs trailed off into blanks. She turned to the woman next to her. What was she supposed to do about the missing parts?

Fill it in as best she could, came the answer.

But what if the missing part was the crucial part? What if it was the section that saved lives? Suddenly, responsibility sat heavy on Sarah's shoulders. She'd asked for more important work. Well, here it was. "At that moment, I resolved not to falter," she said.

30

DECEPTION, PURE AND SIMPLE

The Allies were ready to invade Italy. To do so, however, they first had to seize the island of Sicily, located south of the Italian peninsula. Once under their control, Sicily would serve as a base from which to launch an invasion of the mainland. Problem was, Italian and German forces knew the Allies would be coming. An attack on Sicily simply made good strategic sense. In anticipation of this invasion, Hitler was sure to reinforce the island's defenses, unless . . . Could they fool the Germans about where the next Allied military operation objective would be?

MI5 agents working on the "Double Cross System" believed they could. And they had a plan—an elaborate one. They took a dead body and disguised it as that of a staff officer named "Major William Martin." There was no *real* Major Martin. Agents made up his entire identity. They outfitted his uniform with service ribbons. They put fake love letters and theater ticket stubs in the pockets. They chained a locked briefcase to his wrist that contained bogus plans for the Allied invasion of Sicily. On April 30, they released the body by submarine off the coast of Spain. Then the Double Cross agents waited. Would the body be found? Would the documents be passed to the Germans? And most importantly, would the Germans be fooled by the false plans?

In the Cottage, Mavis monitored the Abwehr Enigma for any mention of "Major Martin." She paid particular attention to messages sent by Nazi spies in Spain. From these she learned the body *had* been found. She learned that the Spanish government *had* shared the discovery with German High Command. But what about those bogus invasion plans? Mavis didn't find a single mention of them.

In the days that followed, the Spanish government returned "Major Martin's" briefcase to the British. Spanish diplomats claimed it had gone untouched. No one had read the documents inside. But a microscopic examination of the papers revealed they *had* been read. By Nazi spies in Spain? If so, had they passed the plans on to Berlin?

On May 14, a long Abwehr intercept landed in Mavis's wire basket. She began cracking it. She got one wheel position, then a second, and finally a third and fourth. She stood and walked over to the Typex machine. She set it up with the wheel positions she'd uncovered and began typing in the enciphered text. Slowly, the deciphered text, now printed onto a strip of white tape, unspooled. It was in German. Mavis began separating the clumps of German into words. The message was from an Abwehr officer in Berlin to his spies in Spain. And what did he say? The German High Command considered the documents to be completely genuine. Mavis must have whooped. The Nazis had been completely taken in by the deception.

ANN

ood heavens, what would she *do*!

Here it was, June of 1943, and twenty-year-old Ann Williamson had given little thought to the war. Instead, she'd been focused on school, grades, and . . . mathematics! Ann loved math's order, logic, and elegance. She lived for a dusty chalkboard full of equations, and could happily spend days solving formulae. She hadn't been surprised when Oxford University admitted her—just one of five females in their mathematics department. She'd always felt she belonged there. A keen student, she'd worked hard. The war, with its rationing and making do, had merely served as background to Ann's aspirations.

But now she'd completed her degree, and the war loomed. The

law required that she do some sort of war work. But what? "I didn't want to go into uniform," said Ann. "I thought it would be horrible to wear [one] and march up and down the drill."

She asked the university to help. Administrators there knew her. Could they recommend Ann to a job that would be stimulating and challenging? Oh, and if possible, she preferred one involving math.

The administrators pulled some strings. "I'm now applying for a temporary assistant in the Foreign Office at Bletchley," Ann wrote in her diary. She was familiar with the name of the place. Many of her Oxford colleagues had ended up working there. Doing what, she didn't know, but it appeared Bletchley was a place for mathematicians.

A month later, officials summoned Ann to the Park for a twenty-minute interview. She met with a staff officer who told her all about shifts, leaves, and billeting. He detailed the Park's working conditions, and outlined its social activities. But when she left, she had no idea what her job actually was . . . *if* they wanted her, that is, and *if* she passed the Park's security checks.

Days passed, and Ann began to worry. Would she end up a Wren, after all? It took three weeks before officials confirmed her position. They ordered her to arrive on September 28.

Ann didn't feel nervous that first day. But she was curious. She grew more intrigued after a staff officer lectured her about secrecy. "Gosh! What secrets this place contains," Ann wrote in her diary that evening, "terribly thrilling, important and vital." After signing the Official Secrets Act, the officer escorted her to Hut 6.

Ann worked in this long, narrow room in Hut 6 (Block D).

Ann must have wondered why they called the place a hut. Seven months earlier, the Hut 6 section had been moved from its original wooden structure to a much larger concrete building known as Block D. Confusingly, it still called itself Hut 6. So did the other huts that moved into the warren-like structure—Huts 3, 6, and 8. Those who'd complained about the wooden structures grumbled even more about the block building. "Cheerless, dimly lit, framed by walls of bare mortar, Block D had more in common with a [hospital] than an office in wartime," remarked one staff member. "In all truth, our new block was a bit of a dump."

Their newest recruit didn't seem to notice. Ann's math skills had landed her in the Machine Room. Right next door, cryptographers worked on finding cribs that might get them into that day's Enigma settings.

When a potential crib was found, cryptographers placed it on a table that sat in the doorway between them and the Machine Room. It was Ann's job to convert the crib and cipher text into a diagram. This diagram, with its seemingly confusing array of numbers, letters, and linking vertical and horizontal lines, specified how the Bombe machines should be set up. They looked like this:

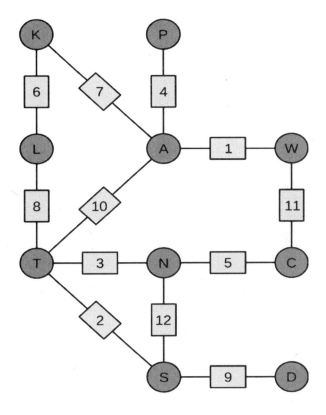

Menu making was the perfect job for Ann's puzzle-solving mind. Hers were "enjoyable days," she wrote in her diary. And because she worked best under pressure, she thrived in the Machine Room. It was a frenzied race to package cribs into tight, workable menus that delivered Bombe stops. And Ann relished every minute. "I worked like the devil," she wrote in her diary. "Good fun!"

Finished menus were placed in a wire basket. "Menus up!" Ann shouted.

Then the head of the Watch—sometimes Ann herself—telephoned the menu to a Bombe outstation. Some of these calls went to Wavendon Manor, or one of the other places where dozens of Bombes clattered day and night. But by the end of 1943, most calls went to Eastcote.

32

THE EASTCOTE WRENS

What did Diana Payne earn after months of working in an airless hut with dripping sweat, dripping machine oil, and the Bombes clattering in her ears?

Another transfer.

This time she headed to Eastcote, an outstation located in the northwest suburbs of London. "It was," said Diana, "a very different set-up after the casual country life [of Wavendon Manor]." Here sat two brand-new, purpose-built Ministry of Defense block buildings. High walls and barbed wire surrounded the buildings. Armed military police stood at the gates. Naval rules and etiquette were strictly observed.

Marching across the parade ground, Diana paused to salute the "quarterdeck" (officers' quarters) before entering the Block A building. The Wrens lived here in a series of rooms, called "cabins." Each was named after a British warship or air carrier. Diana's cabin, HMS *Formidable*, was made to hold thirty-six pairs of bunk beds. None, however, had yet been assembled. So the young women built the bunks themselves. "No good complaining," recalled one Wren. "You just had to get on and make the best of it." Within the year, Block A would house eight hundred Wrens.

At Eastcote, the Wrens did all the work. They mopped the "decks" (floors), served food in the "mess" (dining room), and scrubbed the "galley" (kitchen). Additionally, they were required to train, drill, and march per navy regulations. Even after an eight-hour shift, Diana would find herself marching around the parade ground in freezing cold and rain. All the while, she longed for hot food and bed.

Block B housed the Bombes—103 of them! Its high, curtain-covered windows made it impossible for anyone to peek in. Its thick, soundproof walls muffled bangs and thumps so the machines couldn't be heard from outside. And an armed guard kept anyone but approved personnel from slipping inside. Eastcote was both secret and secure. But all these precautions made the atmosphere inside gloomy and airless. And it was so loud, some Wrens suffered permanent hearing loss.

Block B was divided into eight rooms called "bays," each containing ten Bombes. Each bay was named after a country occupied by the Nazis, and each Bombe was named after a city in that country. To her surprise, toward the end of the year, nineteen-year-old Diana was promoted, and put in charge of one of the bays. Instead of operating a Bombe, she now kept track of which Enigma ciphers were being run, and which Wrens were running them. More importantly, she drew out the menus for distribution.

Bombes at the Eastcote Outstation. The women are sitting at checking machine stations.

On a scrambled telephone line, Bletchley Park was patched through to Eastcote. The head of the Watch from each hut spoke directly with the bay supervisor. Was it possible that Diana spoke with Ann? She may have, although neither identified themselves by name for security's sake. The Watch head gave Diana a detailed description of the menu. Listening closely, Diana inserted the menu letters in the correct places with the horizontal, vertical, and diagonal linking lines between the letters in the correct places. She worked meticulously. One mistake and the Bombes would never locate the correct settings. Precious time and resources would be wasted, and lives might be lost. With the diagram created, Diana distributed them. Soon the Bombes clattered away.

If one of them found settings that checked out, Diana called back the Watch head. She would say something like, "Hello, this is Norway supervisor. I've a good stop for you on Oslo." She then relayed the stops. On the other end, the head of the Watch—maybe even Ann—took them all down.

It was stressful work with long hours, and Diana felt the strain. She developed stomach ailments. If only she could escape the base on her off-hours. London was so close she could have gotten there in minutes on the tube. Or, if she wasn't in the mood for the bustling city, she could have simply strolled across Lime Street to a pub, a shop, or the cinema. Eastcote was in an urban area, after all. But officials prohibited this. They'd established what they called an "eight-mile exclusion zone," meaning the Wrens couldn't frequent any businesses within eight miles from the center of the base. This rule was intended to reduce loose talk. But it ended up making the Eastcote Wrens feel imprisoned. They were—for the most part—high-spirited, energetic teenagers (two-thirds of the Eastcote Wrens were between seventeen and twenty years of age) who longed for fun. Instead, they were stuck in a large machine room in northwest London day after day. What was it all for?

Higher-ups knew the girls often felt demoralized. And so every few weeks, they would bring all the Wrens together and give them a talk. This talk might convey (without specifics) how the work they'd done a few weeks earlier had enabled an Allied success somewhere in Europe or the Atlantic. Or it might allude to a certain set of Bombe-deciphered messages that had resulted in the sinking of an Italian cruiser, or the bombing of an armaments supply train in France.

These talks boosted morale. They provided meaning to

the repetitive and exhausting shift work, and gave the Wrens purpose for their long hours on base. Knowing their efforts had helped in the battle against the Nazis, even in a small way, kept them going. Diana clung to this knowledge. It made all the monotony and misery worth it.

33

INVASION OF SICILY

In July—eight weeks after the Abwehr confirmed that Berlin had been taken in by the Major Martin ruse—Allied forces attacked the southern tip of Sicily. They met little resistance. That's because most of the Italian and German troops were waiting for an invasion of the north coast—exactly where Martin's fake documents had said it would occur. By the time Nazi commanders realized they'd been deceived, the battle for Sicily was nearly over. By mid-August, Allied forces largely had control of the island, and had begun shelling the mainland.

On September 8, Mavis and Keith headed to the movie theater. Two months earlier, top brass—realizing the cryptographer was a far better cipher breaker than airplane pilot—had called Keith back to Bletchley Park. He'd been angry about it at first. But Keith was practical and analytical. He understood the importance of his work. He'd put aside his anger, and buckled down. His return, of course, had overjoyed Mavis. And it had sharpened her focus even more. Together, she vowed, they'd defeat the Nazis . . . one intercept at a time.

This map of Sicily, mounted in the White House War Room, showed the Allied forces plan of attack.

An American cargo ship is hit by a bomb during the invasion of Sicily.

Now, as the couple took their seats, a newsreel filled the screen.

"Surrender in Italy," screamed its caption. The announcer came on. "The Italian government has surrendered its own forces unconditionally," he exclaimed.

Once again, Mavis glowed with secret pride. She'd had a part in this extraordinary victory. Too bad no one would ever know. Not even Keith.

34

FRONT ROW VIEW OF THE WAR

In November, Patricia Owtram transferred to the Y station at Abbot's Cliff in Kent. A bleak, gray house that had been a private home before the war, it perched on a cliff top halfway between the towns of Folkestone and Dover. From its watchtower, Patricia could look across to the coast of France and the cliffs of Cap Gris-Nez just twenty-three miles away. She could see its lighthouse and cluster of whitewashed houses, and on a bright day, the flashes of sunlight reflected off car windshields. If Patricia looked through the station's large telescope, she could even read the time on the clock tower in Nazi-occupied Calais.

This proximity exposed the Y station to enemy attack. Every few days, shells lobbed from a German battery across the English Channel rained down on the countryside. Siren warnings blared and people raced for cover. Sometimes even Patricia and her colleagues headed for the air raid shelter if the bombardment was close enough.

The British military had responded by building elaborate defense works—pillboxes, trenches, and minefields. Rows of birch poles, their ends sharpened into spears, had been set up in the fields behind the cliffs to deter German gliders from landing while Allied antiaircraft guns pounded away at enemy planes flying overhead. Nearby sat a ruined airfield where burned-up planes stood in skeletal rows, bombed out months earlier by the Luftwaffe.

The Y station, too, had been fortified. Great coils of barbed wire surrounded the property, and military policemen guarded it around the clock. The fifty young women who worked there, including Patricia, were instructed on how to use submachine guns . . . just in case. They also had weekly evacuation drills. In case of Nazi invasion, each young woman was expected to disable her radio before setting it on fire. All paperwork—intercepts, orders, red forms—would also be fed to the flames. Nothing could be allowed to fall into enemy hands. Only when all sensitive material had been destroyed could the women head for the safety of the Allied bunkers.

One day, shortly after she arrived, Patricia was in the watchtower when a German long gun fired on a merchant ship moving through the Channel. Instantly, the ship—part of an Allied convoy—burst into flames. Had anyone survived? Gripped with worry, she looked through the telescope and scanned the choppy water. Only debris floated on the surface. As for the convoy, it had continued moving westward, leaving the wounded ship drifting alone. "It was a moment none of us [in the watchtower] would ever forget," Patricia later said.

If You Were a Code and Cipher Breaker: Enciphering a Cipher

What is a teleprinter? It's a machine that sends and receives printed messages via telephone cables or radio relay systems. The teleprinter—which looks very much like a typewriter—was once the most common way of quickly sending information across long distances. News agencies used them. So did local telegraph offices and other businesses. To send a message, a teleprinter operator simply types on the machine's keyboard. Each keystroke generates a sequence of coded electrical impulses that are sent to their destination. The receiving teleprinter decodes the incoming pulses and prints the message onto paper.

All teleprinters use a common code system. There is nothing secret about it and it is used internationally. Called the Baudot-Murray Code (although it is not a code, but rather a cipher), it is named after its inventors, and represents each letter of the alphabet by a series of five electrical pulses. Each series of impulses, appearing in varying configurations, stands for one letter. An electrical impulse is either "on" or "off." On is written as an X; off as a dot. Here is the teleprinter code:

A: X X * * *   N: * * X X *

B: X * * X X   O: * * * X X

C: * X X X *   P: * X X * X

D: X * * X *   Q: X X X * X

E: X * * * *   R: * X * X *

F: X * X X *   S: X * X * *

G: * X * X X   T: * * * * X

H: * * X * X   U: X X X * *

I: * X X * X   V: * X X X X

J: X X * X *   W: X X * * X

K: X X X X *   X: X * X X X

L: * X * * X   Y: X * X * X

M:* * X X X   Z: X * * * X

In a message, the letters are written vertically like this:

A	B	C
X	X	*
X	*	X
*	*	X
*	X	X
*	X	*

Imagine you are sending the word HELP by teleprinter code. It would look this this:

*	X	*	*
*	*	X	X
X	*	*	X
*	*	*	*
X	*	X	X

Since HELP is written in the internationally known teleprinter code, anyone could decode your message. Obviously, you wouldn't choose this method of communication if you wanted to send secrets. But what if you *did* want to send classified information using a teleprinter? How would you do it?

The Nazis have figured out a way. They've begun encrypting the Baudot-Murray Code, by using a cipher machine called the Lorenz SZ40/42. The Lorenz machine is attached to the teleprinter. When the operator types a message at the teleprinter's keyboard, the stream of electrical impulses generated by the teleprinter passes through the Lorenz cipher machine. The Lorenz enciphers the original letter by adding a different letter to it. These randomly generated letters are called **keys.**

Say, for example, the Germans wanted to send the letter C. In Baudot-Murray Code that would be:

*

X

X

X

*

What the Lorenz machine would do was randomly generate a letter like M. In Baudot-Murray Code that would be:

*
*
X
X
X

The Lorenz machine would then add those two letters together. How? By following these simple rules:

Dot + Dot = Dot

X + X = X

Dot + X = X

X + Dot = X

Now, let's try adding the key letter M to our message letter C using the above rules. Remember, the sum of these two letters will be the cipher letter. Ready?

C		M		Cipher text
&ast;	+	&ast;	=	&ast;
X	+	&ast;	=	X
X	+	X	=	&ast;
X	+	X	=	&ast;
&ast;	+	X	=	X

The sum of C + M = * X * * X

Using the teleprinter code above, we can easily decode the cipher text:

$$* X * * X = L$$

L is the cipher text, and it is the letter that will be sent via teleprinter, obscuring the message letter C.

The Lorenz SZ40/42 creates cipher text for *every single letter* in *every single message*. No wonder the German High Command thinks Lorenz-encrypted messages are unbreakable. But are they?

1944

D-DAY AND
ITS SECRET HELPERS

35

BY LEAPS AND BOUNDS
AND A SECRET BUILDING

By 1944, Bletchley Park was deciphering some twenty-five hundred army and air force messages every single day, as well as two thousand naval communications. Most of the staff working on them had no idea they were cracking Enigma ciphers. The Park had effectively become a factory production line. Each girl—whether listening in at a Y station, running a Bombe machine, or clicking away on a Typex—performed the same, single job day in and day out. Each did her job efficiently. More importantly, she did it unquestioningly.

Almost seven thousand people now worked at the Park. Three-quarters of them were young women, and most were under twenty-one. Wrens, WAAFs, and civilians billeted together, shared meals in the canteens, rode bicycles in the countryside on their days off, laughed, and cried. They went to the tea hut, to the social clubs, and even to the hair salon that had just been set up inside the Park. They also went to the newly established "sun ray clinic." Dozens of women had complained about the lack of natural light in their workplaces. It was, they claimed, ruining their health. Park officials responded by providing staff with the chance to lie under ultraviolet lamps in their off-hours.

Concrete-block buildings continued to spring up. The Cottage, where Mavis worked, was absorbed into Block G with its cement floors and brick walls. A fluorescent light flickered overhead, and there was so much dust that her papers always felt gritty. No matter how cramped and drafty, the Cottage had felt like home. Block G felt like a factory.

Construction had also begun on a massive, steel-reinforced building. Why did Bletchley Park need something like *that*? Its purpose, of course, was shrouded in secrecy. Of the thousands who worked at the Park, only a handful would ever learn its true purpose.

36

ELECTRIFYING NEWS

Just after the New Year, the Hut 4 supervisor called his staff together for a meeting.

As Sarah headed for his office, her nerves jangled. Had he learned she'd nicked someone's sweet ration to buy a chocolate bar? Was she getting the axe? She took a seat, preparing for the worst.

"The Allies [are] going to invade France in six months' time," said the supervisor.

Instantly, Sarah's nervousness vanished. Hope took its place.

Her supervisor continued. The goal was to push Hitler's troops back into Germany. Along the way, Western Allied troops would liberate France, as well as other Nazi-occupied countries.

Top secret plans were already underway. But the run-up to invasion—known as D-Day—was bound to cause a flood of intercepts. Did the Germans expect an Allied attack? Where did they think it would come from? Were they preparing, and if so, how? Imagine if the Allies had the answers to these questions in advance of the invasion. It could make the difference between success and failure. It could save lives. And so he was asking them to work longer, harder, and faster. The Allies needed this vital intelligence.

Now came a stern reminder. Secrecy was paramount. "Do not share this news. Do not talk about it, even among yourselves. Loose lips cost lives."

Sarah left the office feeling electrified. "Restlessness vanished," she recalled. "Excitement and exhilaration took its place." She returned to work with renewed purpose. "From [then] on every German decrypt had a broader significance," she said. Now she saw their contents as a "shaft of light to guide our forces to their ultimate objective."

37

PREPARING THE WAY FOR D-DAY

Throughout the spring, British and American air forces set out to cripple the Luftwaffe. Invasion plans called for Allied troops to land on French beaches. The Nazis were sure to counter an invasion with an aerial attack . . . *unless* they were put out of commission. And so a massive bombing campaign began. The skies over Europe grew dark with clouds of Allied bomber planes. They blew up German airfields and airplane factories, while long-range fighter planes took to the sky to shoot down Nazi aircraft.

Luftwaffe intercepts poured into Hut 6 as the Germans reported to each other about the damage being inflicted.

At her Typex machine, Jane Hughes read them all. She was

learning the Nazis' movements even before Bomber Command (which controlled the Royal Air Force).

An aerial view taken by Allied bomber planes in April 1944 shows them hitting their German targets.

The Nazis would surely have been shocked to learn that a twenty-year-old British debutante knew so much about the Luftwaffe's movements. Did they ever suspect a break in their Enigma cipher? It didn't appear so. Every day, Luftwaffe officers grew more frustrated, more fragmented, and more frantic. They communicated all of this via Enigma.

FISH

Cryptographers at Bletchley Park code-named them FISH: encrypted messages containing the most important, top-level Nazi secrets. Hitler and others in the German High Command used FISH to communicate with their top generals and field marshals across Europe. These communications contained reports and assessments, detailed battle plans, and orders from Hitler himself. They revealed the enemy's strategic thinking, planning, and decision-making. Y stations had been intercepting FISH messages since 1940. Frustratingly, few of them could be broken into.

That's because FISH messages were enciphered using a new, secure, and more complex machine—the Lorenz SZ40/42.

Unlike Enigma, which had three (sometimes four) wheels and created enciphered messages using the twenty-six-letter alphabet, Lorenz had twelve wheels and enciphered messages using a series of electrical impulses. These messages were sent by a teleprinter (to which the Lorenz machine was attached). As long as the receiving end also had a similar machine, and knew that day's wheel settings, the secret message could easily be revealed. Like Enigma, the Germans changed the Lorenz settings every day. So advanced was the Lorenz SZ40/42 that it could send out a message with around 100 trillion trillion trillion trillion googol different start possibilities (compared with Enigma's 159 quintillion). Hitler called Lorenz SZ his "secret writer." He had complete confidence in it.

At Bletchley Park, cryptographers worked nonstop trying to break into the FISH intercepts. But they were doing it by hand, and it often took four to six weeks to work out the settings. By that time the information gleaned from them was too old to be of much use. They had to find a way to speed things up.

It required ingenious insight, brilliant inspiration, and laborious work. But finally, in early 1944, a technological marvel was born: Colossus, the world's first-ever electronic computer.

A "Tunny" Machine, the British code name for the German Lorenz SZ40/42, on current display at Bletchley Park.

Colossus didn't resemble a modern-day computer. The size of a room and weighing a ton, it looked like some sort of crazy contraption "held together with elastic and bits of strings," remarked one of its designers. But it was fast, able to read five thousand characters per second with its electronic eye. Even though its job was to work out just the first half of a FISH setting (the second half was still broken by hand), it reduced the time to break a FISH message from weeks to sometimes just hours.

COLOSSUS
BACK VIEW

THYRATRON
'RINGS'

FIG. 3

COLOSSUS

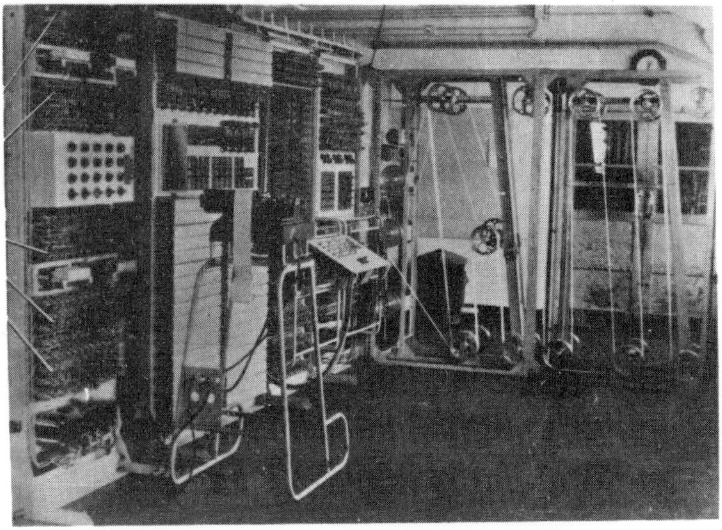

COUNTERS

FIG. 4

COLOSSUS

'WESTAT'
POWER SUPPLY
EACH UNIT
50V D.C.OUTPUT

FIG.5.

A series of three images labeling the various parts of Colossus.

All that spring, Colossus whirred away in Block F. Despite its speed, a single machine could not crack all the FISH intercepts arriving at the Park. Between February and June, two thousand such messages arrived, but cryptologists only had the capabilities to tackle 10 percent of them. Frustratingly, they were forced to prioritize. Which lines of communication would produce the best intelligence? Cryptologists had identified fifty-five different FISH links between Berlin and its far-flung military. They gave each of these links the code name of a different fish. The most important links—and ones on which cryptographers chose to focus—were between Hitler and the German commander in France (code-named Jellyfish), and between Hitler and the German commander in Italy (code-named Bream).

From Jellyfish and Bream they reaped extraordinary information. In the weeks leading up to D-Day, they learned the precise number of German troops in France, as well as the complete tallies of *all* their equipment—from pistols to tanks and trucks. Astonishingly, a Jellyfish link carried all the conversations between Hitler and his commander in France, including the commander's plans for defense against Allied invasion, and Hitler's changes to those plans.

The Führer's plan left weak points in the Nazis' defense, a vulnerability Allied commanders would be able to exploit.

Thrilled by what FISH was revealing, and eager to decipher even more, Colossus engineers made a few improvements to their original design, then ordered the construction of a second machine. By June 1, Colossus II whirred away next to its prototype.

39

SURPRISE VISITORS

Just outside the tower door at Abbot's Cliff Listening Station, Patricia Owtram yawned and stretched in the early morning sunlight. It had been an especially busy night shift. Patricia sensed something was going on. Something big. She could tell by the increased German radio chatter. And last night had been the busiest yet. Her fingers ached from hours of frenzied transcribing, and her eyes burned with fatigue. She needed sleep, but first, some fresh air.

The May sun felt warm on her face as she headed down the path toward the cliffs. She hadn't gone far, however, when she saw a small group of army officers walking in her direction. Patricia did a double take. The man in the middle looked very familiar. Could it be? No, she told herself. She must be dreaming, or hallucinating. After all, it *had* been an intense night shift.

The men drew closer.

And Patricia gasped. It was! The man in the middle was Prime Minister Winston Churchill. And beside him walked Field Marshal Bernard Montgomery, commander of all Allied ground forces. What should she do?

Navy rules required servicepersons to salute a senior officer, but only when wearing a proper uniform. Patricia, however, wasn't wearing one. She had on a pair of blue jeans and a pull-over sweater, as allowed on the night shift.

The men came closer.

"Um . . . uh . . . good morning!" she cried, giving them a wave.

"Good morning," the men replied. They walked on.

Patricia stared after them. What were they doing in *here*, and so early in the morning? Something was definitely up.

She didn't know that Churchill's appearance was part of Operation Fortitude, yet another complicated and top secret plan to fool the Nazis. The Germans knew the Allies would eventually invade Europe. They just didn't know where and when. The Allies wanted to keep it that way. And so, for the past several months, they'd embarked on a deception

Prime Minister Winston Churchill (left) with Field Marshal Bernard Montgomery (right), c. 1944.

campaign to convince the Germans that the invasion would come via France at the Pas de Calais region, the shortest and most obvious route across the English Channel. A variety of ruses had been used. Among them was fake radio traffic sent over the airwaves. This traffic—helpfully intercepted by the Nazis—detailed bogus Allied plans to invade the Calais area sometime in mid-July 1944. Additionally, under the Double Cross System (German spies turned MI5), double agents in Britain were feeding even more false information to Berlin; information that supported the fake air traffic.

Now as Churchill and Montgomery walked along the cliffs, they *tried* to be conspicuous. They wanted German spies across the Channel to report their presence back to Berlin. They hoped Nazi intelligence would see their visit as more evidence supporting an Allied invasion at Pas de Calais, a port city that just happened to be directly across the English Channel from Abbot's Cliff Listening Station.

With luck, the Nazis would take the bait and never learn the true site of the Allied invasion: five Normandy beaches—Utah, Omaha, Juno, Gold, and Sword—located 160 miles northeast of Calais.

40

THE POET IN HUT 10

Gwen Davies still toiled over low-grade ciphers in Hut 10. After two years, the job had become a slogging bore. Thank goodness for her colleagues. They were so different from anyone she had known in her prewar life. There was Denys Webster, lover of Italian opera. He sang them so loudly and so often that soon Gwen, too, knew parts of the arias.

There was Maurice Zarb, who "spoke more languages than he could remember," and read voraciously in all of them. He talked to Gwen about Russian novels, Eastern love poetry, and Mozart—topics she'd never discussed before. "Conversation with Maurice was like being fed with delicious and fascinating food," recalled Gwen. "You always wanted more of it."

And then there was a mysterious older woman—the only other female in Gwen's department—who wrapped herself in caftans and scarves no matter the weather. She endlessly lamented her "lost happiness," and longed to return to Cambridge, where she'd been a professor. Curiously, Gwen never learned her name. Still, the woman's intellect and eccentricity enthralled her. All her colleagues did. Getting to know them had opened up Gwen to new and endless possibilities. She didn't have to live her life in an ordinary way. She could study Egyptology, or take singing lessons, or . . . She decided to write a novel.

So she was delighted when another writer arrived in her section one spring morning. It was Vernon Watkins, a poet who'd just published his first book with the prestigious publisher Faber and Faber. "[He] came in, walking in a springy way as though on heather," Gwen recalled.

Slight, lithe, and middle-aged, Watkins greeted them by reciting a verse of poetry. Then he laughed, and explained why he was in Hut 10.

Months earlier, he'd been given an officer's commission, but failed miserably. At training camp, he marched his squad into a brick wall, and had forgotten to bring along his rifle.

To make matters worse, his commission interview had gone terribly.

"[The Air Commander] hoped I wouldn't be writing any more poems while serving in the RAF," Vernon told them. "I replied that as a matter of fact I wrote poems all the time, because what poets wrote about war was far more important than what historians wrote."

Denys, Maurice, and the woman professor agreed with him.

Gwen, however, hurried to her seat and scribbled down all she'd just heard. Vernon Watkins had just given her an idea for her novel.

41

PREMONITIONS

Jane Hughes could feel it. Something big was coming. Certainly, no one traded details of their work, but one couldn't mistake the tense, almost feverish excitement in the canteen when the cryptographers sprinted in, bolted disgusting platefuls of kidneys on toast without complaining, and sprinted out, pencils at the ready. Yes, she could feel it. And lots of other workers could, too. Something big was coming.

The decrypts on Sarah Norton's table told the story. The Germans had been busy, laying thousands of naval mines in the Channel. But what was the location of those mines? Vital to the invasion's success would be the minesweepers, whose job it was to clear a safe path for the amphibious vessels filled with troops. Discovering where the explosives lay was vital to the operation. Sarah opened her German dictionary. *Mine . . . floating mine . . . marine mine . . .*

Mavis rarely left her desk these days. Like the rest of the Park, she felt taut and nerve-racked. Were the Germans buying the British deception? Did they think the invasion would take place at Pas de Calais?

The Spy Enigma held the answer.

The minute intercepts arrived, Mavis snatched them up. Her fingers clenched the pencil as she broke into the day's settings. So far, Berlin had swallowed the deception. But the Germans were clever and resourceful. How long before they figured out the truth?

42

THE DAY BEFORE D-DAY

On June 5, Sarah caught the train to London. She'd been given an unexpected forty-eight-hour leave, and after weeks of frantic work, she was ready for some fun. Still, as she squeezed into a soldier-crammed train compartment, she felt unsettled. The invasion was sure to happen any day now. "I felt fearful and fretful," admitted Sarah, "although I could not have told anyone the reason for it."

That evening, she met a date at the Berkeley Hotel for dinner. Despite the laughter, conversation, and food "as good as it could be with rationing," Sarah couldn't stay focused. Her mind kept wandering to the invasion. "I tried to quench my unease."

It was eleven thirty when they left. To her dismay, it was pouring outside. Her date popped open an umbrella and the two huddled beneath it.

Suddenly, there came a sound. "At first it was a distant hum, and then a low murmuring with monstrous intensity," recalled Sarah. It grew louder and louder. Above them, the already dark sky grew even darker as more than a thousand RAF planes flew over London toward the shores of Normandy.

It was the invasion!

"My heart went with them as they flew," said Sarah.

All around, people pointed skyward, amazed and speechless.

"Do you know what is going on?" her date asked her.

"I haven't the faintest," replied Sarah, hoping she sounded truthful.

Then she gave her date a quick kiss on the cheek and hurried away. Still wearing her evening dress, she caught the four a.m. train back to Bletchley Park. "I thought I had better get back to work," she said. "With an invasion on, those German naval signals were sure to pile up."

After all, a single translation could mean the difference between life and death.

43

WATCHING AND LISTENING

At Abbot's Cliff Listening Station, Patricia Owtram was shaken awake.

"It's started!" shouted her roommate.

Patricia knew instantly what "it" was. Despite all the military's secrecy, she'd known the invasion of France was imminent. In the days and weeks prior, there had been a buildup of troops in the area, and in Folkstone, "you couldn't walk down the road without having to jump on the pavement to let a tank pass," she recalled. From the watchtower she'd seen all kinds of ships moving toward Portsmouth Harbor—destroyers, landing craft, minesweepers, and something that looked like an upside-down table with long, spindly legs. Later she would learn that this was a temporary, prefabricated floating harbor. Placed just off the coast, it would help Allied forces off-load troops and cargo onto France's beaches.

Throwing on her clothes, Patricia rushed to the watchtower. The room was full of senior naval officers. "If we needed any clue of the importance of the day, this was it," she said.

Joining the crowd at the windows, they looked out across the gray and misty channel. A convoy of landing craft headed across the choppy water. Was it her imagination, or could she see the helmeted heads of the troops? "I thought of the young servicemen I'd met and laughed with at dances and parties, parachuting or sailing into unimaginable danger," she later recalled. So many young men would die in this undertaking. She whispered a prayer.

44

D-DAY

The wind was blowing hard as the convoys of amphibious landing craft made their way toward Omaha Beach. All over the sea, boats crawled toward France. Each carried Allied troops, packed shoulder to shoulder. Men going into battle. The battleship USS *Texas* shelled the shore. From the decks of their vessels, troops could see the heat-bright flash of the ship's big guns and the smoke that pushed out against the wind and blew away. A moment later, onshore, a tower of black earth and smoke marked where the shell had landed. All the shrubbery and gorse on the beach burned. The wind kept the smoke from these fires close to the ground, obscuring the battle already raging from those just arriving.

Soldiers crammed into a landing craft head for the beaches of Normandy.

A priest says Mass aboard a British warship before launching the men into harm's way.

The Enigma Girls

As the landing craft drew close to the beach, it lowered its ramp. The men waited. Each wore a hundred-pound pack on his back, containing weapons and ammunition wrapped in waterproof coverings. The signal came, and the men ran down the ramp into waist-high water. They waded to shore. They were attempting a frontal assault in broad daylight against a beach littered with land mines and defended by a dug-in enemy. There was no place for the troops to take cover. No boulders or trees to duck behind. They would be running directly into Nazi bullets. Already, the sea churned red with blood, and the beach was littered with bodies. Machine gun fire pelted the sand and antitank shells whistled overhead. The troops hit the sand. Behind them, even more men were coming—wave after wave of them.

That day, June 6, 1944, some 156,000 American, British, and Canadian troops landed on five beaches along a fifty-mile stretch of coast in France's Normandy region. The British and Canadians met light opposition as they stormed Gold, Juno, and Sword Beaches. The Americans tasked with taking Utah Beach also met with light resistance. But on Omaha Beach, US troops faced heavy resistance. Eventually, after a tough and bloody fight, they, too, successfully stormed the beach.

Allied soldiers battle their way from the landing craft to the beach.

An injured soldier on the beach at Normandy.

Day turned to night. Allied troops braced themselves for what they believed would be an inevitable and massive German counterattack. But hours passed and the counterattack never materialized. The troops could hardly believe it.

Having gained the safety of the cliffs at their backs, American troops take a breather. They've secured the beach, but the battle's far from over. Soon these men will begin pushing across France toward Germany.

Little did they know that because of Britain's deception and Bletchley Park's intelligence, Hitler believed the invasion was a ruse meant to distract his army from the "real" attack at Pas de Calais. And so he refused to move several key German units held in reserve there. Instead, reinforcements came from farther away, causing delays.

Fighting continued for the next five days. But by June 11, less than a week after storming the Normandy coastline, Western Allied troops had all five beaches fully secured. It came at a heavy cost. In that five-day span, American casualties totaled 124,394: 20,668 killed, 10,128 missing, and 93,598 wounded. Casualties for British and Canadian troops were placed at 83,945: 15,995 killed, 9,054 missing, and 57,996 wounded. Germany, too, suffered a terrible loss—a staggering 290,000 casualties: 23,000 dead, 67,000 wounded, and 200,000 missing or captured.

D-Day was the biggest land invasion in history. And it was the first step toward pushing Hitler's army back into Germany.

45

THE GIRLS AT TROOPS' SIDES

For five long nights, the battle for Normandy's beaches raged in Patricia Owtram's earphones. Gone was the empty hiss of static and the cat-and-mouse games. Now the air was thick with the dot and dash of Morse code. Patricia grabbed them. Intercepts piled up, the stacks rushed to Station X.

In the Hut 6 Machine Room, Ann Williamson concentrated on diagramming the cribs. Her world shrank. Nothing else mattered. Lines, letters, and numbers formed in her mind and flowed out through her pencil. "Menus up!" she called again and again. "Menus up!"

*   *   *

Next door in the Decoding Room, Jane Hughes's fingers flew over the keys of her Typex machine. She didn't try to read what came out. There wasn't time. Her eyes burned. Her mind felt sanded. She kept going.

At Eastcote, the Bombes crunched through Enigma ciphers. Diana Payne could not leave her bay. She could not slack off. Every wheel change; every plug-in; everything was urgent. The sound of a "stop" made her heart leap. Did it check out? Diana grabbed the scrambler phone to call it in. So many people, so many lives depended on them.

In Hut 3, Sarah Norton translated like mad.

German to English.

German to English.

She felt like she was in a trance.

And still the decrypts poured in.

Almost five thousand Enigma messages a day were intercepted during the five-day battle for Normandy's beaches.

Incredibly, each of these intercepts was deciphered, translated, and forwarded to Allied commanders within *half an hour* of arriving at Bletchley Park!

The enemy never suspected a thing.

46

JOANNA

At the end of June, a bus pulled up to the Park's gates, and twenty Wrens dressed in crisp white blouses and navy-blue skirts climbed off. They paused at the guardhouse so military policemen could check their identity cards before following a naval officer to the mansion's oak-paneled ballroom. There they heard an ominous lecture about loose lips, before signing the Official Secrets Act. Then they were escorted to Block F.

Inside the windowless building, eighteen-year-old Joanna Chorley stopped in her tracks. Ticking away at the end of the corridor was an enormous machine "with tapes going around . . . and values and transistors and flippy-flappy things. It was like magic and science combined," she remembered.

It was Colossus I.

Joanna was instantly drawn to it. "When I saw [it], I thought, this is what I want to do."

The enormous success of the computers had led to the construction of even more—by the end of the year, another eight would arrive at the Park. Park officers planned to expand the whole process of deciphering FISH into what was effectively a factory production line (much as they did with the Bombe and Enigma codes). To achieve this, 273 Wrens were deployed to Bletchley Park. They would operate the Colossi in shifts around the clock. Some toiled in Block F, while others—like Joanna—found themselves in the newly completed, steel-reinforced Block H.

When FISH messages came into Block H from the Y stations, they were first printed out on punched-paper teletype tape. Next, Wrens prepared them for Colossus by taking two identical tapes and splicing them together to make a loop. This loop would run through the computer repeatedly.

The loop was handed over to the computer operators. Colossus needed two Wrens plus a cryptographer who worked out how the computer should be programmed.

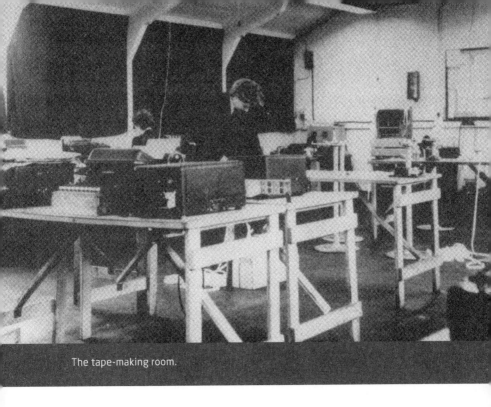

The tape-making room.

Under his direction (all the cryptographers in Block H were male), Joanna and her partner plugged cords into a pegboard located on the machine's back. This was called "pegging the wheel," and to Joanna's dismay, every time she put in a plug, Colossus gave her an electric shock. "But I did love the beast," she said. "And I was determined to look after it, and make life easy for it."

Next, the Wrens set the wheels around which the tape was placed. Finally, they slipped the tape behind the computer's photoelectric eye. "You had to be sure its little eye was clean or it wouldn't be able to see," recalled Joanna. Then they

A pair of Wrens minister to the needs of a Colossus.

carefully adjusted the tape's tension. Too tight, and it would snap; too loose and Colossus would turn it into a paper snarl.

At the front of the machine were buttons, switches, and dials. The Wrens pushed some and flipped others according to the cryptographer's directions. Then Joanna started up the machine.

Colossus whirred.

The Wrens waited. "You would know if you got a positive result," said Joanna. "It would tell you. It would go click click click whizz, and the tapes would all run down."

Colossus found the first half of the FISH settings. But the second half still needed to be discovered. And so Colossus's results went to Block F, where a four-man team of cryptographers used paper and pencil to crack the second half by hand. Once they'd broken in and knew the complete setting, they passed them on to Room 27.

Here sat fourteen "emulators," specially built machines that replicated the Nazis' Lorenz-attached teleprinter. Members of the ATS (Auxiliary Territorial Service, the women's branch of the British army) operated these emulators. First, they entered the settings—a complex process of plugging metal pins into a switchboard-like contraption. Then they typed the enciphered messages into the machine. If the settings were worked out correctly, German text printed out. Recalled one ATS emulator operator, "the gentle clack of the machines became the background to our working lives."

The intelligence produced by the emulators went to Hut 3 for translation and analysis. And it was extraordinary stuff. All that summer, as the Western Allied troops fought their way out of Normandy and across France, FISH revealed Nazi battle plans. It revealed something else, too—the increasing desperation of Hitler and his generals.

47

GWEN AND VERNON

On the last Sunday in June—just weeks after D-Day—Vernon Watkins invited Gwen Davies to the village fair. Over the past weeks, the poet had come to admire her intelligence and good humor. He kept his feelings to himself, though, barely speaking to her during their shifts. No wonder she'd been surprised by his invitation. Still, the weather was lovely and she adored fairs, so she agreed to go along.

Now, the two strolled past food and game stalls and stopped to admire the blue ribbon-winning sheep. By the time they headed back to the Park for the late shift, the night sky was speckled with stars.

Suddenly, Vernon cried, "Wait a minute!"

Gwen stopped.

"You know we have to get married," he exclaimed.

"Oh? No!" she replied. "I mean . . . Vernon, I really don't want to get married. I'm only twenty-one."

Vernon realized he wasn't making himself clear. He tried again. "No, I mean *we* have to get married."

Gwen couldn't believe her ears. Up to now, Vernon had never indicated he liked her in that way. Besides, at thirty-six, he was so *old*.

"Well, Vernon," she stuttered, "I'm very fond of you, but . . ."

Vernon interrupted her. "Yes," he said, as if answering his question for her.

"It was so strange, so sudden," Gwen later recalled.

Somehow, the two returned to the Park without Gwen ever giving an answer.

But that didn't stop Vernon from heading to London the next time he had leave. He returned to Hut 10 with an engagement ring.

"I was overwhelmed," admitted Gwen. "I was a little working class girl . . . what in heaven's name had made him do this?"

Then again, why shouldn't she marry Vernon? "I knew he was a very good man. So I thought, all right, I am not actually in love with him, but I am never going to get a chance [to marry a poet] again. Never."

So Gwen said yes to Vernon, and farewell to what she'd come to fear most—a plodding and ordinary future.

（48）

FIGHTING ACROSS EUROPE

After pouring onto the beaches at Normandy, Western Allied troops fought to drive the Nazis back across France. On August 25, 1944, they liberated Paris. Eight days later, on September 2, they crossed the Belgium border, freeing a large majority of the country—including the cities of Antwerp and Brussels—in just ten days. Then they crossed into the Netherlands. The liberation of that country began. Meanwhile, the US Fifth Armored Division reached the tiny country of Luxembourg. It took just five hours to wrest it from the Nazis. It happened so fast, soldiers barely had time to realize what they'd done. Allied troops sat on the German border!

Victorious American troops march down Paris's most well-known street, the Champs-Élysées, to shouts of joy from Parisians. Behind them, symbolically, is the Arc de Triomphe.

They marched toward the German town of Aachen. For twenty days—from October 2 to October 21—the two sides slugged it out. Hitler vowed to fight to the last man. But in the end, German troops surrendered. Western Allied troops were now poised to push toward the Rhine River and into the very heart of Germany.

These G.I.s didn't know it, but they weren't fighting alone. Every one of their maneuvers was matched—by Patricia's keen ears and Jane's clicking teletype keys; by Mavis's cipher breaking and Gwen's word games; by Sarah's translation skills and Ann's complex menus; by Joanna's devotion to Colossus and Diana's cantankerous Bombes as they clacked their way to vital "stops."

American G.I.s snap a photo of the Eiffel Tower in almost the same spot as Hitler took his photograph four years earlier.

On Monday, September 4, 1944—the day *after* British troops liberated Brussels, Belgium—citizens flocked to this city square to celebrate.

(49)

OCTOBER BRINGS CHANGES

In October, Gwen Davies and Vernon Watkins dashed off to London on a forty-eight-hour leave. Together, they stood in the chapel at St. Bartholomew Church. Shafts of sunlight beamed through the stained-glass windows, bathing the bride in a multicolored glow.

Gwen looked lovely. She'd saved up her ration coupons so she would have enough fabric for a new dress—a pale green one with a matching hat. Her mother and sister-in-law had sewn feverishly to get it made on time. She also clutched a bouquet of roses. Where had Vernon found such an extravagance?

After the service, the little wedding party went to lunch at the Charing Cross Hotel. "Ham, salad, wine and meringues," remembered Gwen. "It was quite well done."

Then the couple took a train to St. Albans, a tiny town north of London, where they strolled through ancient Roman ruins and sprawling parks. Vernon recited poetry. Gwen began to fall in love with him.

All too soon, they returned to Bletchley. The newlyweds billeted in the village with an elderly widow who treated them like her own family. And every day, they went to work together in Hut 10.

That same month, Sarah Norton found herself in Commander Travis's office. He was transferring her to the Admiralty. She was expected in London immediately.

Stunned by the suddenness of it all, Sarah wandered into Hut 4 to say goodbye to her colleagues. "It was a painful departure, and many tears were shed . . . mostly by me," she said. Then she turned and walked away, passing for the last time through the Park's front gates. Hours later, she climbed onto the train. She carried the same suitcase and teddy bear with which she'd arrived, but not her gramophone. She'd left that behind for her friends.

*　　*　　*

October brought changes to Abbot's Cliff, too. That month, the listening station was disbanded. Its main purpose had been to listen for German naval traffic in the English Channel. But since D-Day, that traffic was silent. Patricia listened as German radio stations closed down with dramatic messages like: "*Auf wiedersehen für immer*" (Goodbye forever). Soon military units arrived to cart off the equipment, and Patricia and her colleagues packed up their duffel bags. They'd been assigned new jobs.

Like Sarah, Patricia found herself in the Admiralty. At a creaky desk in a tiny office, she spent long hours typing up deathly dull technical documents. One was about the wiring of a German U-boat. Another detailed the types of land mines. It all made Patricia yawn.

In truth, she missed the excitement of a busy night at the Y station. She'd spent years in the thick of the action. Was this her future now?

50

MARION AND CHARLOTTE

arion Graham arrived at Bletchley Park on a gray November day. Plucked from secretarial school by the Foreign Office just after her eighteenth birthday, she now found herself in Japanese Section I in Block F. In a cramped office along with three other young women, she typed up Japanese messages that would eventually be shared with American cryptographers in Washington, DC. These messages, already decrypted and translated into English, were mostly about Imperial Japanese troop movements.

Since the attack on Pearl Harbor, a small team of Bletchley Park cryptographers had been trying to master Imperial Japan's many encryption systems. Still, most of the Park's resources went toward deciphering German messages. Germany, after all, was Britain's immediate menace. Besides, the United States had taken the lead on breaking into Japan's ciphers. Why spend long hours duplicating work already done by the Americans?

But after D-Day, with Germany seemingly on the run, Bletchley Park's top brass felt confident devoting more resources to Imperial Japan's ciphers. Working closely with the Americans, they retrained members who'd been working on German ciphers, and enlisted new recruits. Marion

While some blocks required renovation or were demolished, Block B—shown here—looks much as it did when built in 1942.

was part of this buildup, arriving at the peak of Block F's growth.

Private Charlotte Vine-Stevens of the ATS arrived in Block F, too. The twenty-year-old had been working as an indexer in an upstairs office of the mansion. But now her job was paraphrasing translated Japanese messages. "I have no idea why [officials] picked me for the job," she later said. But Charlotte quickly discovered she was good at it.

For example, a translated, intercepted message might read:

Troops of 3rd Battalion will be moved to attack Kohima in 3 days time

Charlotte would paraphrase it to read:

Expect Kohima to be attacked 3 days from now by battalion strength

These paraphrased messages would then be transmitted by radio to commanders in the field.

Why paraphrase? Because British intelligence worried that Japanese listeners would intercept *their* transmissions. If that happened, the changed wording might disguise the fact that the Japanese cipher had been broken. The enemy would not be able to determine with certainty where the intelligence had come from—broken cipher or another source?

A Japanese rotor machine used to encrypt messages.

"I enjoyed getting my teeth into more 'meaty' work," said Charlotte. Her head stuffed with secrets, she returned to the ATS military camp each night. Did anyone else know what she did? If they did, like her, they could not say a word.

(51)

DECEMBER'S BLOODY BATTLE

O n the snowy morning of December 16, 1944, Hitler launched a surprise attack. Nearly two hundred thousand German troops struck in the Ardennes Forest—a seventy-five-mile stretch of dense woods in Belgium. It was a weak spot in the Allied front. Just four battalions of inexperienced and battle-exhausted Americans had been stationed there. After a day's hard fight, the Germans broke through the front. They seized key crossroads and crucial bridges. They cut Allied communication lines. Fearing the worst, the Belgians—who just months earlier had welcomed American troops—took down their Allied flags and brought out their swastikas. In Paris, French citizens quaked at the thought of the Nazis' return. Even British generals, who'd thought final victory was near, were sobered by this sudden Nazi onslaught.

Allied reinforcements rushed to counterattack. On Christmas Day, an American armored division stopped the advancement of enemy tanks. But the battle raged on into the middle of January. Again and again, Western Allied forces attacked. Again and again, the Germans fell back. At long last, battered and depleted, the Nazis retreated into Germany, and the Allied front on the German border was restored. The stage was set for the final drive to victory.

1945

WAR'S END AND THE YEARS AFTER

52

BLAME GAME

Bletchley Park found itself being blamed for failing to give warning of Hitler's surprise attack in the Ardennes. How could they have failed to pick up the movements of fourteen infantry and seven Panzer divisions along a seventy-five-mile front? Surely, Abwehr and its Spy Enigma had buzzed about it. So how had Mavis missed it? And what about FISH? Surely, Hitler had communicated with his commanders in the field using these links. How could something this big have slipped through the cracks? Some in the military labeled the event as "the most notorious military intelligence disaster of the war."

Bletchley Park's top brass defended themselves. Yes, they *had* picked up word of an imminent attack. They'd even known its date. But nowhere in the decrypts had the location been specified. They might have learned more if they'd had more to work with. But fewer and fewer German Enigma messages were being intercepted. The reason for this was simple: As Nazi troops shrank back into Germany, they had less need for radio communications. No longer were Hitler's soldiers stretched across Europe. Most were now within Germany's borders, and using landlines. And what had once been a surge of Enigma traffic had given way to a trickle.

53

FAREWELL, GWEN

That same month, Gwen Davies Watkins said goodbye to her friends in Hut 10. She felt both sad and angry. It didn't seem fair. But what could she do? She'd been discharged from the WAAFs because she was pregnant. "I was sorry to leave," admitted Gwen. "I hoped I could stay working at Bletchley until I nearly had the baby."

She'd even argued her case to Commander Travis. Couldn't he keep her on as a civilian? Didn't he need her decoding skills?

But Travis stood firm: No expectant mothers at the Park. Gwen grumbled about his decision. It seemed absurd. Was he afraid she'd go into labor on the job? "Heaven forbid an ambulance might have to come through the gates!" she exclaimed.

Now she waited—for Vernon's return to their billet each day; for the birth of their baby; but above all for the end of this long and dreadful war.

54

BEGINNING OF THE END

That spring, the army of the Soviet Union fought its way eastward, driving German troops out of Poland . . . then Hungary . . . then Austria. By mid-April, the Soviets stood just miles from Berlin, poised for battle.

Meanwhile, the Western Allied forces fanned out and overran all of western Germany, from the Baltic Sea in the north to the Bavarian Alps in the south. They, too, pushed on toward Berlin.

In Block H, Joanna Chorley found herself working nonstop. With Enigma messages dwindling, FISH communication now produced the best intelligence. And it revealed an increasingly frantic Hitler, and a German military in chaos.

The Enigma Girls

An overturned Nazi tank lies in a shallow German stream.

German soldiers captured in the Ruhr area, a major industrial region in western Germany.

A young and fearful German soldier is captured by Allied troops.

Indeed, the Colossi were doing more work than ever, reaching their peak output in March, the same month Allied forces crossed the Rhine River. FISH traffic became almost more than the section could cope with. At the end of each shift, Joanna stumbled back to her billet and dropped exhausted into her bunk. But she returned the next day eager to start again. She thrived on adrenaline and hope. And she saw every whir and whistle of Colossus as another nail in Hitler's coffin.

55

SILENCE!

In mid-April, Commander Edward Travis sent a memo to all heads of staff. Any decrypts detailing the enemy's final days must be restricted, he warned them. Workers could be told *nothing*. No matter how euphoric the news. Travis worried the staff wouldn't be able to keep the secret. But sealed lips remained imperative. There was still the war in the Pacific. They didn't want to tip off the Japanese to their intelligence operation, did they?

The end seemed near. Months earlier, Adolf Hitler had withdrawn to an underground bunker beneath the chancellery in Berlin. Here he met with generals and gave orders. But as the Soviet army grew closer, Hitler grew more frantic.

Finally, on April 30, with the Soviets just half a mile from his bunker, he committed suicide.

The news arrived via FISH within hours. Once decrypted, it spread like wildfire.

Joanna Chorley was on shift when a woman burst into Block H and shouted the news. The entire section cheered. But Joanna and others couldn't contain their excitement. Running into the restroom, they grabbed up rolls of toilet paper and raced outside. They were laughing and flinging streamers of tissue over the just-leafing branches of a large tree when Travis stormed out of the mansion.

"What are you doing?" he cried. "This is dreadful! Shut up! Go back to work!"

The girls laughed all the way back to their stations.

(56)

VICTORY IN EUROPE

On the evening of May 7, Sarah Norton sat in her tiny office at the Admiralty. The telephone rang. She picked up the receiver. "Will you go over?" asked an official from Bletchley Park. This was code. The official wanted to make sure Sarah was on the scrambler phone, used for secret conversations. Sarah assured him she was, and he tersely reported the news. The Germans had surrendered.

The news made for a very busy night. Not until early the next morning, as Sarah walked home through London's still-quiet streets, did she have time to examine her emotions. Too tired to be deliriously happy, she "just felt a deep contentment," she admitted.

Then, as she crossed Trafalgar Square, church bells began

to peal out all over the city. Londoners had not heard those bells for five-and-a-half nightmarish years. But now, at long last, they rang out again, a symbol, said Sarah, of "endurance, and faith in victory."

Prime Minister Churchill declared May 8 a national holiday. Like so many others, Joanna Chorley squeezed onto the train bound for London. There, jubilant crowds thronged the street. People hung from lampposts, kissed strangers, swam in the fountains, danced and hugged and cried.

Joanna headed to Buckingham Palace. But the pavilion

VE Day celebration in London's Trafalgar Square.

was packed. She couldn't see a thing. So the eighteen-year-old scrambled up onto an immense bronze lion. With her skirt hiked up and her legs wrapped around the statue's neck, she cheered along with the crowd as King George waved from the balcony and Prime Minister Churchill flashed his famous V sign. It was thrilling.

It was also impossible to get down. Joanna slipped and clutched at the statue. She almost fell. Luckily, a pair of American G.I.s offered a hand. With her feet once more planted on the pavement, she gave each a kiss on the cheek. After all, it *was* VE Day (Victory in Europe Day). If a girl couldn't kiss a G.I. then, when could she?

Ann Williamson went to London, too. With her Kodak Brownie Box Camera, she made her way through a sea of revelers and ticker tape, snapping photographs. As day gave way to night, the city's lights snapped on. After years of blackouts, London was once again lit up. Ann gazed at Admiralty Arch bathed in floodlight. It looked glorious!

Patricia Owtram was also in London. But rather than elbow her way through crowded streets, she stayed inside to listen to King George's radio address:

There is great comfort in the thought that years of darkness and danger . . . are over and, please God, forever. We shall have failed and the blood of our dearest will have flowed in vain if the victory which they died to win does not lead to a lasting peace founded on justice and good will.

To that, then, let us turn our thoughts on this day of just triumph and proud sorrow; and then take up our work again, resolved as a people to do nothing unworthy of those who died for us and to make the world such a world as they would have desired, for their children and for ours.

"It was a wonderful moment," Patricia recalled, "like a collective exhalation at the end of a long period when we'd all been holding our breath."

Marion Graham and Charlotte Vine-Stevens remained on shift at Bletchley Park. Nothing could stop them from having some sort of celebration, though. All the staff from all the blocks gathered on the lawn in front of the mansion to listen to the king's broadcast. They cheered and hugged. But Marion and Charlotte's delight felt muted. The war with Japan continued. So once the radio snapped off, they returned to Block F. There were decrypts to type, and messages to paraphrase.

*　　*　　*

At Eastcote, Diana Payne "began to feel that this strange life of secrecy would never end," she confessed. "But suddenly, Germany crumbled and the Bombes fell idle and quiet."

No more menus came through from Bletchley Park.

Instead, orders to dismantle the Bombes arrived just twenty-four hours after the VE Day celebration. Top brass wanted nothing to remain of the machines. No one must ever learn that they'd been breaking Enigma ciphers, or how they'd done it.

Bombe operators took apart the machines wire by wire and screw by screw. Did Diana experience mixed emotions as she pulled them apart? The machine had been the source of so much difficulty. Running it had made her physically ill. Unfortunately, Diana did not record her thoughts about this, but another Bombe operator did. "We sat at tables with screwdrivers taking out all the wire contact brushes. It had been a sin to drop a drum, but now we were allowed to roll one across the floor . . . Whoopee!"

The Bombe Wrens were out of work, but they were still in the navy. Some went to new stations and different jobs. Most, however, went home. There were no debriefing sessions.

Besides a final stern warning about secrecy and silence, they were turned back out into the world.

Diana never got a "thank you" for her service. But she didn't need one. She knew the Bombe operators had made a huge impact on the war's outcome. Yes, the brains at Bletchley Park had made brilliant discoveries. But the success of those discoveries, she reminded herself, "was dependent on the unremitting toil and endurance of almost two thousand Wrens."

57

LEAVINGS

The number of workers at Bletchley Park began to "sort of dribble down," recalled one worker. As spring turned to summer, more and more people walked out through the Park's gates. But *not* before being reminded of their pledge to secrecy. They couldn't breathe a word about their war work. Not ever.

In late May, Ann Williamson left Hut 6. She felt unnerved by the abrupt loss of the work she'd loved. Now what? Even with a mathematics degree from Oxford, she couldn't get an engrossing, challenging job. That's because women were being turned out of their wartime positions to make way for returning servicemen. In fact, they were being encouraged to return to the domestic sphere. But Ann wasn't ready to be

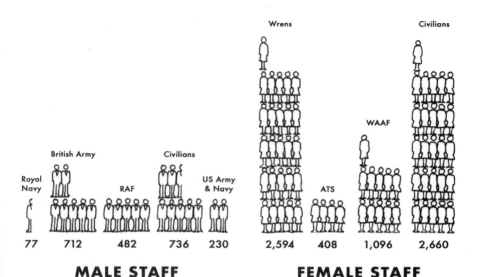

JANUARY 1945

	Royal Navy	British Army	RAF	Civilians	US Army & Navy
	77	712	482	736	230

MALE STAFF

Wrens	ATS	WAAF	Civilians
2,594	408	1,096	2,660

FEMALE STAFF

By war's end, far more women than men worked at Bletchley Park, and most of them were Wrens, as this chart shows.

someone's wife . . . or mother. Eventually, she found a job at Oxford's Bodleian Library.

That same month, Jane Hughes also left the Park. She was headed to London to take a three-months-long crash course in Japanese. Afterward, top brass expected her to return and translate Japanese decrypts.

Charlotte Vine-Stevens left in May, too. To her complete surprise, she'd been reassigned to Washington, DC. Reporting for duty in the newly built Pentagon building, she was tasked with paraphrasing intercepted Japanese communications—the same job she'd done at Bletchley Park. "The constant flow of signals between Japanese forces kept me busy," she recalled.

Joanna Chorley departed in July after top brass ordered all but two of the Colossi dismantled. Luckily, Joanna wasn't part of the team tasked with doing it. She loved the computers too much. But she did slip one last time into Block F to say goodbye to them. "I was told I could take a part of one of them with me," recalled Joanna. She pried off a switch. "I kept it for years."

Who remained at the Park?

Mavis still worked in Block G. But now, instead of the Abwehr Enigma, she pitted her brilliant mind against Russian ciphers and codes. Was it possible she could stay on at the Government Code & Cipher School? Might she have a career as a cryptographer? She hoped so.

Meanwhile, for those still at the Park who were *not* breaking ciphers, a massive cleanup operation got underway. The sprawling Index—tended so carefully for so long—was shredded. So, too, were billeting records, requisition orders, even copies of canteen menus. It was essential that every trace of their work disappear. Finally, teams of workers went through each building not in use. On hands and knees, they searched for every scrap of code and cipher. Huge bonfires consumed paperwork. Soon, all that remained were empty huts and memories.

58

VICTORY IN JAPAN

On the morning of August 6, 1945, American forces dropped an atomic bomb on the Japanese city of Hiroshima. According to modern-day scientists, the number of people killed by the impact is "fundamentally unknowable" because of differing evidence. However, most scholars agree that between 70,000 and 140,000 Japanese women, children, and men lost their lives that day. Scores more were injured, and 60 percent of the city was flattened.

In Block F, Japanese Section, staff understood what had happened long before the news became public. Said one young woman, "You could tell from the disruption of all the messages that something terrible had happened. You could just hear the people standing there screaming their heads off."

An atomic cloud rises over the Japanese city of Nagasaki.

The wrecked framework of the Museum of Science and Industry in Hiroshima as it looked just after the first atomic bomb was dropped.

Three days later, on August 9, a second bomb was dropped, this time on the Japanese city Nagasaki. Another 40,000 to 70,000 people were killed, and thousands more injured. Nagasaki, too, was decimated.

Those working in the Japanese Section had yet to grasp the full horror of the bomb, or its lasting effects on generations. "At the end of a long war," said Charlotte, "it simply meant we were winning."

Marion Graham and four others were on duty the afternoon of August 14. Their superior officer, Commander

Williams, came into the room. "The signal has been intercepted from Tokyo to Geneva," he said.

"The Japanese are surrendering." The news, he went on, had just been forwarded to the prime minister.

The girls didn't whoop or cheer. They simply sat in silence. After six years . . . was it truly, finally over?

Williams didn't seem to know what to do, either. He shuffled about and then blurted, "Well, you better get on with your work now."

At shift's end, Marion returned to her billet. She hadn't heard another word about the surrender. Had it been a dream? But as she stepped through the front door, her landlady shouted, "We've just heard the war's over!"

Marion couldn't say, "I know." Instead she simply replied, "Oh, how wonderful."

But for the rest of her life she would hug that moment close. It was a secret she couldn't share with anyone. She'd sworn an oath. But it was "a great moment," she said. She had been one of the very first people in the world to know the war had finally ended.

On August 15, British streets once again swarmed with revelers, this time celebrating V-J Day (Victory in Japan Day). In

London, there were proclamations, royal appearances, bonfires, and fireworks.

Across the Atlantic Ocean in Washington, DC, "Everyone went crazy," recalled Charlotte. Horns blared. People shouted and waved. She joined a crowd that thronged toward the White House calling, "We want Harry! [Harry Truman, president of the United States.] America just erupted, went mad!"

And in a small hospital tucked away in the British countryside, Gwen Watkins Davies gave birth to a baby girl. How incredible! After six years of bloodshed and struggle, her daughter was born into a world *without* war.

A jubilant crowd on V-J Day dancing on the White House lawn.

59

HUSH-HUSH

They never said a word. Not any of them. For thirty years, they stayed silent.

Mavis went on to break ciphers for the GC&CS until 1947, but kept her work entirely hush-hush.

Jane became an opera singer—famous, photographed, and admired. Yet her lips remained sealed.

Patricia worked as a journalist, covering some of the biggest news stories of the late twentieth century. But not a word did she let slip about her life as a secret listener.

Charlotte remained in uniform until 1970. She kept her oath and kept mum.

Sarah sparkled in society. She became a viscountess—the

toast of the British peerage—but not a whisper escaped about her war work.

Gwen and Vernon moved to Wales. Although they'd worked together in Hut 10, they never spoke to each other about their time there. It was as though their work never happened.

As for Ann, Marion, Diana, and Joanna, they each married and raised families. But they never once hinted to their husbands about their work at Bletchley Park. They didn't talk about it to their children. And if their grandchildren asked, "What did *you* do in the war, Grandma?" they lied. They said they'd been writers or typists. "This explanation did not always satisfy," recalled Diana, "so my wartime activities were considered unimportant and something of a failure." Still, they'd vowed to stay silent, and they did.

But secrets can't remain buried forever.

In the 1970s, a handful of books about Bletchley Park trickled out. Based almost entirely on memory and conjecture, they generated little public interest. Then in 1977, the British government released seventy thousand intelligence documents related to the work done at the Park. Here was solid evidence! Journalists and historians sifted through the mountain of material. And slowly, the remarkable story came to light . . . and it seized the public's imagination. The trickle of books became a river. Suddenly, there were documentaries, radio programs, magazine articles, and more.

Bletchley Park itself, with its random clutch of huts and blocks, sat crumbling. After the war, the place had become home to a variety of training schools: for teachers, post office workers, air traffic controllers, and telephone engineers. There were moves to demolish the whole site in favor of a supermarket. Luckily, in 1991, a small group of history lovers managed to save the property. They restored huts, built replicas of Bombes and Colossi, filled display cases with historical odds and ends—a Wren's uniform, a ration card, black-and-white photographs of staff at work and play. An Enigma machine received pride of place. Within three years, Bletchley Park opened to the public as a museum.

Mavis visited. So did Jane and Sarah. All of them traveled back at one time or another. Memories came alive as they crunched up the gravel path to the main house. They must have felt surprised by their return. The place, after all, had been built on secrets. Did they take the tour? Did they correct the guide? Or did they stay mum about their pasts? They'd been discreet for so long. They'd never once betrayed a confidence.

The Enigma Girls

"Could we now tell our families why we were so good at anagrams and Scrabble and crossword puzzles?" wondered Mavis.

Diana Payne broke the silence first. "I had buried this part of my life so completely . . . that it was a shock to see the story suddenly shown on television over thirty years later," she said. But now, with the secret out, Diana decided to write an essay about her experiences. Titled "The Bombes," it appeared in *After the Battle* magazine in February 1982. She hoped her story would spotlight the contributions of Wren Bombe operators.

Gwen went next. She'd never finished the novel she'd begun in 1942. But now she wrote her memoir, *Cracking the Luftwaffe Codes*, because she felt slighted by previous books about Bletchley Park. They implied that nothing of importance went on "except the breaking of Enigma codes," she grumbled in her foreword.

Others followed their lead. Charlotte and Patricia wrote about their war experiences. So did Sarah. Mavis, instead of chronicling her own life, chose to write a biography about her friend and mentor Dilly Knox.

Soon, they were all giving interviews and appearing in documentaries. A few—Jane, Mavis, Ann, Joanna, and

Charlotte—even gave talks to fascinated museumgoers who visited Bletchley Park. Joanna was especially thrilled to get a chance to talk about her beloved Colossus. "Every time you use your phone or your baby computer in your hand you are actually using exactly the same things as part of Colossus," she told audiences. "It is still an amazing thing!"

No longer did they have to hide their achievements from their family and friends. No longer did their contributions go unrecognized. At last, they could tell the world how they'd helped break German ciphers and saved Allied lives. Their work, according to some historians, had shortened the war by two entire years.

Said Jane in an interview, "Working at Bletchley Park was the most important thing any of us have ever done in our lives." She paused and gave a little laugh. "We just didn't realize it at the time."

A NOTE ABOUT THE PHOTOGRAPHS

Why aren't there more photographs of Bletchley Park and its staff? For the obvious reason that snapping pictures and keeping secrets don't mix. After 1940, all photography at Bletchley Park was prohibited. Still, some pictures do exist. They can be seen at https://artsandculture.google.com/story/jwXhiZthYm-MJg?hl=en. As for the young women highlighted in this story, since I could not find a photograph of each, I chose not to show any. Besides, it's not how they looked that's important, but rather their inner qualities: intelligence, dedication, courage, and the ability to keep mum.

AUTHOR'S NOTE

I took the train from London's Euston Station to Bletchley. It was the same route Jane had taken ... and Mavis ... and Sarah ... so many years before. In my mind's eye, I saw the train car crowded with soldiers, and a young woman, riding alone, her suitcase on her lap, her eyes full of uncertainty.

At the Bletchley station, I hopped out onto the platform. I didn't need directions. I knew the way. I'd walked it dozens of times with my Enigma girls. The same short gravel path led to the Park. No guards or barbed wire greeted me, though. Security had given way to a museum and gift shop.

It didn't matter. I believe that landscapes speak and houses hold memories. And as I walked the grounds, I could *feel* the past. Here was the mansion headquarters where they pledged themselves to a lifetime of secrecy and silence. Behind it, encircled by a hedgerow, stood the cottages where Mavis broke ciphers and fell in love. Hut 4—Sarah's workplace—still crouched next to the mansion. Did I smell toast? It was likely, since the hut is now a café.

Hut 6 and 3 are standing, too. I walked down the center corridor, poking my head into room after room. The place felt so familiar. I could almost hear Jane's Typex machine clacking away in the Decoding Machine Room; practically see Ann contentedly drawing up menus in the Machine Room.

Sadly, Block F, where Joanna tended Colossus, and Charlotte and Marion worked on Japanese ciphers, is gone now, demolished in 1988. Still, I stood on the spot where it had been and looked across the grounds, imagining them here. I had to imagine Gwen, too. While Block A remains, it has been converted into a permanent exhibition space. Where did Gwen work? I couldn't find the spot. I did, however, see a case displaying a German cipher book. Had Gwen worked with it? I could only hope.

At last, I made my way to Hut 11 and 11A, where the Bombes were first housed. Here, a working model of Diana's "mechanical monsters" churned away. I watched it, perplexed. None of it made sense to me. It looked like nothing but a jumble of leftover parts. How had Diana ever mastered its complexities?

The day was almost over. As I moved toward the entrance, I saw a wireless radio on display. I stared at it. Patricia never visited Station X during the war, but her intercepts—and millions more like them—were the reason for Bletchley Park.

By the time the light faded from the sky, I was headed back to London. I looked out at the Buckinghamshire countryside. Lights winked everywhere, blackouts long forgotten. My mind wandered back to my ten Enigma girls— young women who'd helped outsmart the enemy. No longer would their lives be blanketed in silence. They would not be forgotten.

BIBLIOGRAPHY

PRIMARY SOURCES

BOOKS:

Baring, Sarah. *The Road to Station X: From Debutante Ball to Fighter-Plane Factory to Bletchley Park, a Memoir of One Woman's Journey Through World War Two*. London: Sapere Books, 2020.

Batey, Mavis. *Dilly: The Man Who Broke Enigma*. London: Biteback Publishing Ltd., 2010.

Owtram, Patricia, and Jean Owtram. *Codebreaking Sisters: Our Secret War*. London: Mirror Books, 2020.

Payne, Diana. "The Bombes." In *Codebreakers: The Inside Story of Bletchley Park*, edited by F. H. Hinsley and Alan Stripp, 132–138. Oxford: Oxford University Press, 2015.

Russell-Jones, Mair, and Gethin Russell-Jones. *My Secret Life in Hut Six: One Woman's Experiences at Bletchley Park*. Oxford: Lion Hudson, 2014.

Turing, Alan M., and B. Jack Copeland, ed. *The Essential Turing: Seminal Writings in Computing, Logic, Philosophy, Artificial Intelligence, and Artificial Life: Plus the Secrets of Enigma*. Oxford: Oxford University Press, 2004.

Watkins, Gwen. *Cracking the Luftwaffe Codes: The Secrets of Bletchley Park*. S. Yorkshire: Frontline Books, 2013.

Webb, Charlotte. *Secret Postings: Bletchley Park to the Pentagon*. Worcestershire: Book Tower Publishing, 2011.

OTHER DOCUMENTS AND VIDEOS:

"After the Battle of Cape Matapan (1941)." British Pathé, YouTube video, https://www.youtube.com/watch?v=ZriHdYXShOg.

"Careless Talk Costs Lives." Docsteach, https://www.docsteach.org/documents/document/talk-costs-lives?tmpl=component&print=1.

"E108—Victory in Europe." Bletchley Park Podcast, https://audioboom.com/posts/7577157-e108-victory-in-europe.

"Every Man to His Post, 1940." National Churchill Museum, https://www.nationalchurchillmuseum.org/every-man-to-his-post.html.

"Italy's Surrender Is Celebrated in Allied Nations (1943)." British Pathé, YouTube video, https://www.youtube.com/watch?v=arZvR0fV2IM.

"King George VI Speaks on VE Day (1945)." British Pathé, YouTube video, https://www.youtube.com/watch?v=pWGE_hDujpc.

"Radio Address by Neville Chamberlain, Prime Minister, September 3, 1939." Yale Law School, https://avalon.law.yale.edu/wwii/gb3.asp.

SECONDARY SOURCES

BOOKS:

Clayton, Aileen. *The Enemy Is Listening.* London: Hutchinson, 1980.

Dunlop, Tessa. *The Bletchley Girls: War, Secrecy, Love and Loss: The Women of Bletchley Park Tell Their Story.* London: Hodder & Stoughton, 2015.

Hill, Marion. *Bletchley Park People: Churchill's Geese That Never Cackled.* Gloucestershire: The History Press, 2012.

Hore, Peter. *Bletchley Park's Secret Source: Churchill's Wrens and the Y Service in World War II.* S. Yorkshire: Greenhill Books, 2021.

BIBLIOGRAPHY

Irving, David. *Hitler's War.* New York: Avon Books, 1990.

Koorm, Ronald. *Backing Bletchley: The Codebreaking Outstations, From Eastcote to GCHQ.* Gloucestershire: Amberley Publishing, 2020.

McKay, Sinclair. *The Secret Listeners: The Men and Women Posted Across the World to Intercept the German Codes for Bletchley Park.* London: Aurum Press, 2012.

McKay, Sinclair. *The Secret Lives of Codebreakers: The Men and Women Who Cracked the Enigma Code at Bletchley Park.* New York: Plume, 2010.

Roberts, Captain Jerry. *Lorenz: Breaking Hitler's Top Secret Code at Bletchley Park.* Gloucestershire: The History Press, 2017.

Smith, Michael. *The Debs of Bletchley Park.* London: Aurum Press, 2015.

Stone, Jean. *Mavis Batey: Bletchley Codebreaker, Writer, Gardener, Historian, Conservationist.* Leicestershire: Troubadour Publishing, 2020.

MAGAZINE AND NEWSPAPER ARTICLES:

Grier, Peter. "Pearl Harbor Attack: How Did Winston Churchill React?" *Christian Science Monitor,* December 10, 2009. https://www.csmonitor.com/USA/Politics/Decoder/2015/1207/Pearl-Harbor-attack-How-did-Winston-Churchill-react.

"Joanna Chorley." *#technicianjourney,* April 10, 2019. https://technicianjourney.com/2019/04/10/joanna-chorley/.

Wellerstein, Alex. "Counting the Dead at Hiroshima and Nagasaki." *Bulletin of the Atomic Scientist,* August 4, 2020. https://thebulletin.org/2020/08/counting-the-dead-at-hiroshima-and-nagasaki/.

OTHER DOCUMENTS AND VIDEOS:

"Station X: The Goose That Laid the Golden Eggs." YouTube video, https://www.youtube.com/watch?v=oGDu-rVTMG4&T=2s.

"Station X: The Keys to the Reich." YouTube video, https://www.youtube.com/watch?v=q4sAzLJs1Zc.

"Station X: The Ultra Secret." YouTube video, https://www.youtube.com/watch?v=aJo55KEEhek.

"Station X: The War of the Machines." YouTube video, https://www.youtube.com/watch?v=B9rWodcS3qE.

SOURCE NOTES

CHAPTER 1: WAR!

"This country is at war . . .": "Radio Address by Neville Chamberlain, Prime Minister, September 3, 1939." Yale Law School, https://avalon.law.yale.edu/wwii/gb3.asp.

CHAPTER 2: SECRET LISTENERS

"Can you stay awake . . .": Sinclair McKay, *The Secret Listeners: The Men and Women Posted Across the World to Intercept the German Codes for Bletchley Park* (London: Aurum Press, 2012), 81.

CHAPTER 3: JANE

"Well, Jane, I'm at Bletchley . . .": Michael Smith, *The Debs of Bletchley Park* (London: Aurum Press, 2015), 35.

"suitable girl": ibid.

"What I am going to say . . .": Gwen Watkins, *Cracking the Luftwaffe Codes: The Secrets of Bletchley Park* (S. Yorkshire: Frontline Books, 2013), 69.

"And what work . . .": ibid., 70.

"Good God, girl . . .": ibid.

"This is the Official Secrets Act . . .": ibid., 71.

"If you did . . .": ibid.

"Well, where are you going": Smith, 36.

"Clerical work": Watkins, 71.

"Careless Talk Costs Lives": Docsteach, https://www.docsteach.org/documents/document/talk-costs-lives?tmpl=component&print=1.

"old overcoats tied shut . . .": "Station X: The Keys to the Reich," YouTube video, https://www.youtube.com/watch?v=q4sAzLJs1Zc.

CHAPTER 4: MAVIS

"We've more important duties . . .": ibid.

"War work": ibid.

"We're breaking [ciphers] . . .": Mavis Batey, *Dilly: The Man Who Broke Enigma* (London: Biteback Publishing Ltd., 2010), 105.

"Have a go": ibid.

"I'm afraid it's all . . .": ibid.

"I wish it were": ibid.

"chopped logic": Jean Stone, *Mavis Batey: Bletchley Codebreaker, Writer, Gardener, Historian, Conservationist* (Leicestershire: Troubadour Publishing, 2020), 38.

"Which way does a clock . . .": Batey, 105.

"Clockwise": ibid.

"Oh, no it doesn't . . .": ibid.

CHAPTER 6: BILLETING BLUES

"My landlady was so mean . . .": Marion Hill, *Bletchley Park People: Churchill's Geese That Never Cackled* (Gloucestershire: The History Press, 2012), 105.

"My accommodation was with . . .": ibid., 107.

"My room was above . . .": "Station X: The Keys to the Reich."

"It really was disgusting": Smith, 45.

"I looked after the children . . .": "Station X: The Keys to the Reich."

"My aunt will be coming . . .": ibid.

"You know, you're not the only one . . .": ibid.

CHAPTER 7: BLITZ!

"cruel [and] wanton": "Every Man to his Post, 1940," National Churchill https://www.nationalchurchillmuseum.org/every-man-to-his-post .html

"Got it!": "Station X: The Goose That Laid the Golden Eggs," YouTube video, https://www.youtube.com/watch?v=oGDu-rVTMG4&T=2s.

"all these German bombers . . .": ibid.

"I know you British . . .": Aileen Clayton, *The Enemy Is Listening* (London: Hutchinson, 1980), 125.

"ghost voices": McKay, *The Secret Listeners*, 99.

CHAPTER 8: A MYSTERIOUS SUMMONS

"You are to report . . .": Sarah Baring, *The Road to Station X: From Debutante Ball to Fighter-Plane Factory to Bletchley Park, a Memoir of One Woman's Journey Through World War Two* (London: Sapere Books, 2020), 64.

"What on earth . . .": ibid., 64–65.

"I hear you speak German": "Station X: The Ultra Secret," YouTube video, https://www.youtube.com/watch?v=aJo55KEEhek.

"Its primary purpose . . .": Baring, 67.

"I was cross-referencing . . .": ibid.

CHAPTER 9: X-3

"TODAY 25 . . .": Sinclair McKay, *The Secret Lives of Codebreakers: The Men and Women Who Cracked the Enigma Code at Bletchley Park* (New York: Plume, 2010), 131.

"It was eleven o'clock . . .": ibid.

"With our Navy's brilliant . . .": "After the Battle of Cape Matapan, 1941," British Pathé, YouTube video, https://www.youtube.com/watch?v=ZriHdYXShOg.

"Ladies and gentlemen . . .": ibid.

CHAPTER 10: BY LEAPS AND BOUNDS AND TEA AND TOAST

"indescribably bad": Baring, 95.

"What a waste": ibid.

"I smell toast": ibid., 97.

"Odd pieces of information . . .": ibid., 71.

CHAPTER 11: A VISIT FROM ADMIRAL CUNNINGHAM

"We all thought him . . .": "Station X: The Keys to the Reich."

"We thought it would be . . .": ibid.

CHAPTER 12: FIND THE *BISMARCK*

"INFORMATION RECEIVED GRADED . . .": Smith, 72.

"is melancholy beyond words": David Irving, *Hitler's War* (New York: Avon Books, 1990), 371.

"How awful it was . . .": Smith, 73.

CHAPTER 13: THE GEESE THAT NEVER CACKLE

"You all look very innocent . . .": Stone, 53.

"Boniface": ibid.

"We think you ought to know . . .": Alan M. Turing and B. Jack Copeland, ed., *The Essential Turing: Seminal Writings in Computing, Logic, Philosophy, Artificial Intelligence, and Artificial Life: Plus the Secrets of Enigma* (Oxford: Oxford University Press, 2004), 336.

"Action This Day": ibid., 338.

"Make sure they have . . .": ibid.

CHAPTER 14: THE SPY ENIGMA

"Spy Enigma": Batey, 131.

"Double Cross System": ibid., xxiii.

"*In science* . . .": ibid., 139.

"Everything that has . . .": ibid., 140.

"If two cows . . .": ibid.

"Lobsters": ibid.

"very fine lobster": ibid.

"It was serendipity . . .": Smith, 186.

CHAPTER 15: PEARL HARBOR

"Mr. President . . .": Peter Grier, "Pearl Harbor Attack: How Did Winston Churchill React?" *Christian Science Monitor*, December 10, 2009, https://www.csmonitor.com/USA/Politics/Decoder/2015/1207/Pearl-Harbor-attack-How-did-Winston-Churchill-react.

"We're all in the same . . .": ibid.

"I went to bed . . .": ibid.

CHAPTER 16: LEAP OF FAITH

"Can you keep a secret": Diana Payne, "The Bombes," in *Codebreakers: The Inside Story of Bletchley Park*, eds. F. H. Hinsley and Alan Stripp (Oxford: Oxford University Press, 2015), 167.

"I really don't know": ibid.

"The Wrens get off . . .": ibid.

"shift work . . .": ibid., 171.

"nuts": ibid.

"a leap of faith": ibid.

CHAPTER 17: BY LEAPS AND BOUNDS AND BASKET RIDES

"The rooms were always . . .": Hill, 31.

"It wasn't a rush . . .": ibid.

"I seemed to be growing . . .": Baring, 90.

CHAPTER 18: CIPHERS AND ROMANCE

"So I went over . . .": Smith, 178.

"rather nice": ibid.

"You've dropped your pencil": ibid., 179.

"It was *not* . . .": ibid.

CHAPTER 19: THE BOMBES

"mechanical monsters": Payne, 167.

"They were bronze-colored . . .": ibid., 168.

"I realized then . . .": ibid.

"Job's up": ibid.

"driven her nuts": ibid., 169.

"Working on the monster . . .": ibid., 167.

CHAPTER 20: LISTENING AND TAPPING

"I didn't find it . . .": Patricia Owtram and Jean Owtram, *Codebreaking Sisters: Our Secret War* (London: Mirror Books, 2020), 61.

CHAPTER 22: THE BIGGEST ASYLUM IN BRITAIN

"I bet my [German] . . .": Watkins, 39.

"I think I'm going . . .": ibid.

"Don't put your kit down": ibid., 40.

"Where": ibid.

"Are you going . . .": ibid.

"Well, the van's ready": ibid.

"Can't come in here . . .": ibid., 41.

"Look, . . . I don't know . . .": ibid.

"Somebody will come . . .": ibid.

"And if you want . . .": ibid.

CHAPTER 23: CIPHERS AND WORD GAMES

"I've got an E": "Station X: The Ultra Secret."

"I've got a B": ibid.

"BERICHT": ibid.

"all rather fun . . .": ibid.

CHAPTER 24: SURPRISING NEWS

"You do realize . . .": Batey, 167.

"Well, this one's . . .": ibid.

CHAPTER 25: LOOSE LIPS

"It could sometimes . . .": Mair Russell-Jones and Gethin Russell-Jones, *My Secret Life in Hut 6: One Woman's Experiences at Bletchley Park* (Oxford: Lion Hudson, 2014), 175.

"And I bet . . .": ibid., 185.

"Well, that's very interesting . . .": ibid.

"I cannot believe . . .": ibid., 186.

"We didn't mean . . .": ibid., 187.

"Ladies, let this incident . . .": ibid.

CHAPTER 26: NO ESCAPING THE MONSTERS

"woes": Ronald Koorm, *Backing Bletchley: The Codebreaking Outstations, From Eastcote to GCHQ* (Gloucestershire: Amberley Publishing, 2020), 99.

CHAPTER 27: THE HAPPY COUPLE AND A GRIM REMINDER

"I realized then . . .": "Station X: The Goose That Laid the Golden Eggs."

CHAPTER 28: LEISURE AND LIES

"There were concerts . . .": Hill, 95.

"I am the personal . . .": Baring, 79.

"I drive a four-star . . .": ibid.

"Well, . . . I am the aide . . .": ibid.

"It's a secret . . .": ibid.

"a bit bleary-eyed": ibid.

"a touch overdressed": ibid.

CHAPTER 29: ENDINGS AND BEGINNINGS

"He was skeptical . . .": Batey, 166.

"At that moment . . .": "Station X: The Goose That Laid the Golden Eggs."

CHAPTER 31: ANN

"I didn't want . . .": Tessa Dunlop, *The Bletchley Girls: War, Secrecy, Love and Loss: The Women of Bletchley Park Tell Their Story* (London: Hodder & Stoughton, 2015), loc. 1279.

"I'm now applying . . .": ibid.

"Gosh! What secrets . . .": ibid., loc. 1731.

"Cheerless, dimly lit . . .": Russell-Jones, 180.

"I worked like the devil . . .": Dunlop, loc. 1926.

"Menus up": ibid, loc. 1915.

CHAPTER 32: THE EASTCOTE WRENS

"It was . . . a very different . . .": Payne, 171.

"No good complaining . . .": Koorm, 111.

"Hello, this is Norway . . .": Dunlop, loc. 3454.

"eight-mile exclusion zone": Koorm, 122.

CHAPTER 33: INVASION OF SICILY

"Surrender in Italy": "Italy's Surrender Is Celebrated in Allied Nations," British Pathé, YouTube video, https://www.youtube.com/watch?v=arZvR0fV2IM.

"The Italian government . . .": ibid.

CHAPTER 34: FRONT ROW VIEW OF THE WAR

"It was a moment . . .": Owtram, 139.

CHAPTER 36: ELECTRIFYING NEWS

"The Allies [are] going . . .": Baring, 117.

"Do not share . . .": ibid.

"Restlessness vanished . . .": ibid.

"From [then] on . . .": ibid.

"shaft of light . . .": ibid.

CHAPTER 38: FISH

"secret writer": Captain Jerry Roberts, *Lorenz: Breaking Hitler's Top Secret Code at Bletchley Park* (Gloucestershire: The History Press, 2017), 52.

"held together with . . .": McKay, *The Secret Lives of Codebreakers*, 261.

CHAPTER 39: SURPRISE VISITORS

"Um . . . uh . . . good . . .": Owtram, 148.

"Good morning": ibid.

CHAPTER 40: THE POET IN HUT 10

"spoke more languages . . .": Watkins, 78–79.

"Conversation with Maurice . . .": ibid., 78.

"lost happiness": ibid., 80.

"[He] came in . . .": ibid., 81.

"[The Air Commander] hoped . . .": ibid., 83.

CHAPTER 42: THE DAY BEFORE D-DAY

"I felt fearful . . .": Baring, 126.

"as good as it . . ." : ibid.

"I tried to quench . . .": ibid.

"At first it was . . .": ibid., 127–128.

"My heart went . . .": ibid., 128.

"Do you know . . .": ibid.

"I haven't the faintest": ibid.

"I thought I had better . . .": ibid., 129.

CHAPTER 43: WATCHING AND LISTENING

"It's started": Owtram, 150.

"you couldn't walk . . .": McKay, *The Secret Listeners*, 300.

"If we needed any clue . . .": Owtram, 149.

"I thought of the young . . .": ibid., 150.

CHAPTER 45: THE GIRLS AT TROOPS' SIDES

"Menus up . . .": Dunlop, loc. 1924.

CHAPTER 46: JOANNA

"with tapes going around . . .": "Joanna Chorley," *#technicianjourney*, April 10, 2019, https://technicianjourney.com/2019/04/10/joanna-chorley/.

"When I saw [it] . . .": Dunlop, loc. 2090.

"But I did love . . .": ibid., loc. 2102.

"You had to be sure . . .": ibid., loc. 3476.

"You would know . . .": ibid.

"the gentle clack . . .": "Station X: The War of the Machines," YouTube video, https://youtube.com/watch?v=B9rWodcS3qE.

CHAPTER 47: GWEN AND VERNON

"Wait a minute": Dunlop, loc. 3638.

"You know we have . . .": ibid.

"Oh? No! . . . I mean . . .": ibid.

"No, I mean *we* . . .": ibid.

"Well, Vernon . . .": ibid.

"Yes": ibid.

"It was so strange . . .": ibid., loc. 3652.

"I was overwhelmed . . .": ibid.

"I knew he was . . .": ibid.

CHAPTER 49: OCTOBER BRINGS CHANGES

"Ham, salad, wine . . .": ibid., loc. 3934.

"It was a painful . . .": Baring, 147.

"Auf wiedersehen . . .": Peter Hore, *Bletchley Park's Secret Source: Churchill's Wrens and the Y Service in World War II* (S. Yorkshire: Greenhill Books, 2021), 245.

CHAPTER 50: MARION AND CHARLOTTE

"I have no idea . . .": Charlotte Webb, *Secret Postings: Bletchley Park to the Pentagon* (Worcestershire: Book Tower Publishing, 2011), 40.

"Troops of 3rd Battalion . . .": ibid., 44.

"Expect Kohima . . .": ibid.

"I enjoyed getting . . .": ibid.

CHAPTER 53: FAREWELL, GWEN

"I was sorry . . .": Dunlop, loc. 4073.

"Heaven forbid . . .": ibid.

CHAPTER 55: SILENCE!

"What are you doing . . .": ibid., loc. 4085.

CHAPTER 56: VICTORY IN EUROPE

"Will you go over": Baring, 154.

"just felt a deep contentment": ibid.

"endurance, and faith in victory": ibid., 178.

"There is great comfort . . .": "King George VI Speaks on VE Day, 1945," British Pathé, YouTube video, https://www.youtube.com/watch?v=pWGE_hDujpc.

"It was a wonderful . . .": Owtram, 177.

"began to feel . . .": Payne, 172.

"We sat at tables . . .": Hill, 132.

"was dependent on . . .": Payne, 172.

CHAPTER 57: LEAVINGS

"sort of dribble down": McKay, *The Secret Lives of Codebreakers*, 280.

"The constant flow . . .": Webb, 58.

"I was told I could take . . .": Dunlop, loc. 4310.

CHAPTER 58: VICTORY IN JAPAN

"fundamentally unknowable": Alex Wellerstein, "Counting the Dead at Hiroshima and Nagasaki," August 4, 2020, the bulletin.org/2020/08/counting-the-dead-at-hiroshima-and-nagasaki/post-heading.

"You could tell . . .": Smith, 250.

"At the end . . .": Webb, 62.

"The signal has been . . .": "Station X: The War of the Machines."

"Well, you better . . .": ibid.

"We've just heard . . .": ibid.

"Oh, how wonderful": ibid.

"great moment": ibid.

"Everyone went crazy . . .": Webb, 61.

"We want Harry . . .": ibid.

CHAPTER 59: HUSH-HUSH

"This explanation . . .": Payne, 170.

"Could we now tell . . .": Batey, 128.

"I had buried this part . . .": Payne, 172.

"except the breaking . . .": Watkins, 14.

"Every time you use . . .": Dunlop, loc. 4998.

"Working at Bletchley Park . . .": "E108—Victory in Europe," *Bletchley Park Podcast*, https://audioboom.com/posts/7577157-e108-victory-in-europe.

PHOTOGRAPH AND
ILLUSTRATION CREDITS

Photos ©: x: © Crown Copyright, by kind permission Director GCHQ; 4 top: National Archives; 4 bottom: AP Photo; 6: Illustrated London News Ltd/Mary Evans/www.agefotostock.com; 7: Franklin D. Roosevelt Presidential Library & Museum; 9: The Royal Aeronautical Society (National Aerospa)/www.agefotostock.com; 10: Library of Congress; 14–15: Candace Fleming; 18: piemags/Alamy Stock Photo; 20, 21, 23: Courtesy of the National Cryptologic Museum; 25: Candace Fleming; 36: Northcliffe Collection/ANL/Shutterstock; 37: Franklin D. Roosevelt Presidential Library & Museum; 38: SuperStock/Alamy Stock Photo; 40 top and bottom: Courtesy of the Living Archive MK; 42: Candace Fleming; 45: Onslows/Bournemouth News/Shutterstock; 47, 48, 49, 50: Courtesy of the National Cryptologic Museum; 53: Candace Fleming; 57, 58: Courtesy of the National Cryptologic Museum; 62, 63: National Archives; 70, 71 top: Franklin D. Roosevelt Presidential Library & Museum; 71 bottom: Library of Congress; 72: Franklin D. Roosevelt Presidential Library & Museum; 74–75: SSPL/Bletchley Park Trust/Getty Images; 77: INTERFOTO/Alamy Stock Photo; 89: Library of Congress; 90–91: Historia/Shutterstock; 92: Library of Congress; 93, 96–97, 98: Candace Fleming; 104–105: Historia/Shutterstock; 109: Eric Rohmann;

INDEX

Page numbers in *italics* refer to illustrations.

ACKNOWLEDGMENTS

This book would not have been possible without the invaluable help from the staff who helped me navigate through their oral history interview collection, as well as archivists at the Center for Buckinghamshire Council in Aylesbury, the Milton Keynes Library, and, of course, the Bletchley Park Trust Archives (BPTA) at Bletchley Park. The BPTA, with its transcribed oral history collection, as well as its letters, photographs, and other memorabilia, provided a rich source of material throughout this project.

I am deeply grateful to Patricia Owtram, Jane Hughes, Mavis Batey, Sarah Norton, Diana Payne, Gwen Watkins, Ann Williams, Joanna Chorley, Charlotte Webb, and Marion Graham for sharing their memories, thoughts, and feelings about Bletchley Park in their books, as well as in interviews, speeches, and documentaries. Most of these incredible women are no longer living, but they have left behind an enormous gift. Reading their life stories not only enriched my understanding of the secret world that was Bletchley Park, but also inspired, awed, and beguiled me. To say that

I admire these women is an understatement. They are my heroes.

Thanks must also go to Susan A. Brewer, Emeritus Professor of History at the University of Wisconsin–Stevens Point, for carefully reading the manuscript and making insightful comments.

As always, I'm grateful to Eric Rohmann for once again contributing his talents to one of my projects.

And finally, many thanks to my editor Lisa Sandell for her encouragement and flat-out hard work, as well as to all the people at Scholastic who helped this project come together, especially Cian O'Day for the exacting work of putting together the book's images.

ABOUT THE AUTHOR

Candace Fleming is the versatile and acclaimed author of more than twenty books for children and young adults, including *Crash from Outer Space: Unraveling the Mystery of Flying Saucers, Alien Beings, and Roswell*; *The Curse of the Mummy: Uncovering Tutankhamun's Tomb*; *The Rise and Fall of Charles Lindbergh*, winner of the YALSA Excellence in Nonfiction for Young Adults Award; *Murder Among Friends: How Leopold and Loeb Tried to Commit the Perfect Crime*; the *Los Angeles Times* Book Prize winner and Sibert Honor Book *The Family Romanov: Murder, Rebellion, and the Fall of the Russian Empire*; and *Amelia Lost: The Life and Disappearance of Amelia Earhart*; among many others. She lives outside Chicago and can be found online at candacefleming.com.